A QUESTION OF

by the same author
with Mary Swainson

GILDAS COMMUNICATES
SEVEN INNER JOURNEYS
THE HEALING SPECTRUM

A Question of Guidance

Ruth White

SAFFRON WALDEN
THE C.W. DANIEL COMPANY LIMITED

First Published in Great Britain
by The C.W. Daniel Company Limited
1 Church Path, Saffron Walden
Essex CB10 1JP, England

© Ruth White 1988
ISBN 0 85207 193 0

Production in association with
Book Production Consultants, Cambridge, England
Typeset by Cambridge Photosetting Services in Bembo
Printed and bound by Billings, Worcester

Dedication

To Barbara,
without whom it may never have been written.

Acknowledgements

I am grateful for all the help and support I have received in the preparation of this book. There is not space to mention all who have given words of encouragement or comfort, and raised my spirits when there was not enough space or time for writing, or when the seemingly inevitable 'writers' block' struck. I hope that they will know who they are, and accept this recognition of their contribution to the final product.

My primary acknowledgement must always be to Mary Swainson, for all her patient early work with, and recognition of me and Gildas. (See 'Gildas Communicates'; 'Seven Inner Journeys'; 'The Healing Spectrum'; all by Ruth White and Mary Swainson, and Mary's own book 'The Spirit of Counsel'. All published by The C.W. Daniel Company Ltd.)

I want to thank specifically: The Centre for Transpersonal Psychology, London, (Ian Gordon-Brown and Barbara Somers), for training and inspiration; Lorna St Aubyn, not only for her foreword but for particular help in creating the space to write, and for reading the script; Annie Wilson for help and advice with the script; Nicola, Bepke, and Mary B. for permitting the use of personal material; Mr Jacques Detiger for financial help.

The Assagioli egg diagram on page 19, and referred to throughout this book is after Ferrucci, as used in 'What We May Be', by Pierro Ferrucci. Published by: Thorsons Publishing Group Ltd., Dennington Estate, Wellingborough, Northants, and the diagram is adapted with their permission.

Contents

Preface

Before you begin. . .
May 29th 1988

As you read this book, and perhaps also from its jacket information, you will learn more about me, Ruth, and my contact with Gildas, my discarnate guide. More of my story can be learned from three previous books written jointly with Mary Swainson, and mentioned elsewhere in the text.

When running a workshop I always ask the individuals in a group to introduce themselves. In that introduction I hope that they will not necessarily say 'who' they are, or 'what' they are in outer terms, but will express where they are coming from at that particular moment, and what they are thus bringing to the group with them. So in this brief preface I should like to honour that formula.

As I write this I am sitting at my desk at my home in the South of France. From my window I have a view over vineyards, rolling down to a 'dragon' cliff where evergreen trees grow. The past ten years of my life have been full of change and the joy/pain of growth. I have just finished receiving Gildas' dictation of the conclusion to this book, and am consciously grateful for the series of 'mini miracles', which have enabled me to divide time between being here to write, and my other work.

I suspect that many of you who will read this book are people I have already met. It has been written with all of you in mind. What I want to do now is to get it fully 'born', which means releasing it to the publishers. I do so gladly, and with a sense of contentment and gratitude.

The next book will be about the chakras, and is already beginning to form. This one, the first I have written alone, has been a long time in gestation. I hope the others will follow more quickly. I hope I've got the formula right. To all readers, wherever you are, thank-you for being there.

Bibliography

(in alphabetical order of author)

An Illustrated Encyclopaedia of Symbols, J. C. Cooper, Thames and Hudson.

Dream Power, Ann Faraday, Pan

What We May Be, Piero Ferrucci, Thorsons Publishing Group Ltd.

Dreams, C. G. Jung, Ark Paperbacks

Man and His Symbols, C. G. Jung, Aldus Books Ltd., London.

The Spirit of Counsel, Mary Swainson, The C. W. Daniel Company Ltd.

The Inner Guide Meditation, Edwin C. Steinbrecher, The Aquarian Press

Gildas Communicates, Seven Inner Journeys, The Healing Spectrum, Ruth White and Mary Swainson, The C. W. Daniel Company Ltd.

The Dreamwork Manual, Strephan Kaplan Williams, The Aquarian Press

Foreword

by Lorna St. Aubyn

At a time when an increasing number of people are beginning to receive guidance from either their Higher Self or a discarnate, it is of vital importance that there be sober and down-to-earth teaching on all aspects of this subject. Although it contains so much potential, there is also so much confusion available. Having herself had thirty years experience of discarnate guidance, Ruth White can write not only about the theory of this fascinating subject, but can also bring us a wealth of practical information gleaned from her own life and from the many workshops she has taught. Trained as a counsellor, with the added perspective of transpersonal psychology, her work in this field is rooted in a rare marriage of the spiritual, the psychic and the psychological, which give great depth and wholeness to what she has to say.

For those who have had no access to seminars or individual training there is, I believe, enormous insight and practical help in 'A Question of Guidance'. For those who have already had the opportunity to study guidance, both new material and useful exercises are made available. Many interesting aspects of the subject are discussed in depth, such as how to differentiate between inner and discarnate guidance, each of which has a significant but quite different contribution to make. Another interesting subject which is discussed at length is the whole question of indiscriminate handing over to guidance, a pitfall into which many beginners fall. The relationship between a medium and his/her guide must not be like that of a puppet-like analysand who telephones his analyst before deciding on the colour of his new socks. Guidance is a partnership in which there must be constant questioning and discrimination. The source of someone's guidance, its clarity and its dependability must all be constantly and rigorously tested. Glamour and self-inflation must be recognized and ruthlessly dismissed.

The dangers of over-enthusiasm are also clearly expounded. Without discouraging newcomers Ruth points out that if progress is too rapid, you open yourself to self-deception, possibly even to psychic disturbances and illnesses. A sound, safe plan of work is outlined. The need for psychological stability when working in this area is also heavily emphasized. For each step that one takes on the spiritual and psychic paths, three steps must be made on the psychological one, she warns us.

For many years in our Western civilization, guidance of the kind that is now becoming increasingly accessible has been confined to the very few and even they have usually had to hide their gift, risking anything from ridicule to accusations of witchcraft. It is only very recently that access to guidance could be taught through books or lectures. But now, as we are being given more and more choice and self-responsibility in our lives, so are more of us finding available guidance of a calibre that will make our decisions more far-sighted and universal. To refuse such an offer would be a pity and a waste. Proffered to us willingly, and with love, in order to help both our individual evolution and the planet's safe passage into the New Age, how can we refuse such an opportunity?

Introduction

The important moments of truth or development in life are often triggered at the most unexpected times. Often, as with the incident which started the train of thought of which this book is the direct result, they will come through a question which afterwards brings deep reflection. The moment, I speak of, was in some respects a humourous one.

'What exactly do fairies look like?' asked a friend. My response was quick, if not articulate; 'Well like ordinary fairies of course'. My friend's laughter was also quick, but I caught in it a note of puzzlement, and the kind of separation which can occur when communication is less than it might be. What a rich learning situation there is in that short interchange! My friend was right in her puzzlement. There was also a separation. Yet in another sense my response was accurate. Fairies as I have perceived them often appear in exactly the way in which they are illustrated in fairy tales, or in that delightful flower fairy series now available in cards, notepaper etc., so that in a sense they can be described as 'ordinary' fairies. (They also, in my experience, manifest as light and colour and subtle fast moving energy).

Ever since I can remember I have been subject to more subtle areas of perception than I now know most people to be, so as part of my daily awareness the fairies are normal and 'ordinary' too. My friend was endeavouring to understand a whole new world which was opening up for her; the concept of fairies was still extraordinary for her; that there might be people who perceive them as part of normal daily living, even more extraordinary. My remark about ordinary fairies, although on the one hand funny and setting us laughing, was as extraordinary as the rest of the situation. It emphasized a degree of separation between our worlds of perception, a space where we could not yet meet with any degree of objectivity. That there is some sort of archetypal storehouse of perception which results in many sources making similar representations of fairies is rarely regarded as objectivity!

Suppose we had been discussing a place in the realms which we normally regard as real, objective, solid, slow to change. A cathedral for example, which one of us had visited and the other not. Aspects of the conversation might have been very similar.

The one who had seen it might say, 'Actually, I found it rather ordinary'. The other might remark, 'Oh, I have always understood it to be quite magical. Perhaps one day I shall see it for myself.'

Accepting that the cathedral exists objectively we also accept that we may have quite subjective views of its character. Despite that subjectivity it will remain the same cathedral. If we see a picture or photograph of it, we shall both recognize the place. We do not question that it is there and will remain there, for the one who has not seen it to see at some future opportunity. The fairies, however must remain a subjective experience, because they exist, if at all, in a realm, or a dimension, or on a plane to which we are not all by any means certain of having access. Can that which is subjective in this sense be regarded also as real? Can we acknowledge that reality itself has other dimensions? Can subjective experience be regarded as a reality so that we soften the boundaries between that which we call real, that which we call imagination and that which we call experiental? Can we push against the normal boundaries of perception, so that we can embrace new concepts of reality, which go beyond the objective as it is scientifically defined? I believe that we can and must make this exploration in this present age.

In this book I offer my own experience, and my understanding of how it comes about, in order that others may explore some of the wonders and challenges of these other worlds. My determination to observe and question some of my own processes of perception came from my friend's puzzlement, I felt a need to attempt to bridge the gap which separated us. The present more general interest in these other dimensions shows that many are ready and eager to make the journey. Here is an attempt to help.

This book contains the material which I have developed

in co-operation with Gildas, (my discarnate guide), for use in workshops and seminars which attempt to help in the search for guidance, and which explore the fascinating interface between the realms of psychology, and those of the spiritual and discarnate worlds. The exercises suggested can be followed progressively over a period of time, and many of them deepen with repetition. For some you will need a co-operative partner or friend.

Before embarking on the exercises I do suggest that you read the whole book, in order to set them in context and give a sense of proportion and definition to their practice. The journey can be a demanding one, but it is usually exciting and fulfilling, bringing a new dimension into life and its understanding.

If at any point in the exploration you feel uncertain, I suggest that you seek help, guidance or support from a counsellor or therapist trained in Transpersonal Psychology, or Psychosynthesis.

CHAPTER I

Exploring Sensitivity

When people come for help with their experiences the expressions I most often hear are, 'I don't know where I am any more;' 'Everything is changing'; 'Things don't feel the same any more'; 'I am lost'.

At some point in every exploration made in life there comes the need to refer to a 'map' in order to understand the course and possibilities of the journey. There will often be experience of the subjective kind of which I have spoken in the introduction to this book. In its subjective and personal nature it may not be mapped, and there may be no knowledge of general maps of the territory which give help in seeing the course and pattern of the personal experience.

Most maps of the Psyche, or the territory of our being, come from the world of psychology. In our times there is increasing interest in the field of Transpersonal Psychology. Briefly defined this is the field of psychology which takes particular account of the spiritual and transcendent drives and needs which manifest in life and experience. These areas often contain the keys to healing and wholeness. This psychology then, deals seriously with the spiritual nature of man, seeking to understand the nature of Higher, or God Consciousness within. It explores the area of individual and collective inner spiritual resources, changed states of 'being', etc. Obviously these regions are very near to those of Esoteric Spiritual Exploration. Some, but certainly not all of the terminology may be interchangeable. Looking at aspects of Transpersonal Psychology can help to open up the understanding and evaluation of what I am calling Esoteric Spiritual Exploration, but it is important to recognize that an interface area and uncharted territory are under consideration. (See diagram *A* on page 19). With this recognition comes the realization that maps and theories can help to contain the exploration and to give it shape. They can help towards a concensus of shared knowledge; but ultimately there can only be trust, confidence, and respect for the personal and individual experience, thus releasing true creativity and the wonder of the unique within the collective.

**Diagram A
Interface**

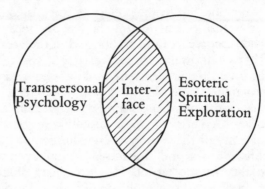

**Diagram B
The Psyche**

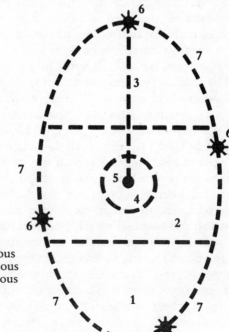

1. Lower Unconscious
2. Middle Unconscious
3. Higher Unconscious
4. Field of Usual Consciousness
5. The ego self
6. Transpersonal or Sun Self.
7. Collective Unconscious

Exponents of what is here defined as Transpersonal Psychology include Carl Jung; Abraham Maslow; William James, and Roberto Assagioli. The most adaptable map I have found to use as a basis for discussion and explanation is the well known egg map of Assagioli. (See diagram *B* on page 19). This is a map of the human psyche, and also of its relationship to the collective unconscious. An important feature of this map is the use of *dotted* lines to denote the boundaries of the psyche and of the areas of being. By the use of the *solid* line, earlier maps of the psyche*, though often in agreement about the areas of being and experience have implied that movement of material from one area to another is more difficult than it necessarily is. In the Assagioli map it should also be noted that the majority of the territory is unconscious. The usual area of consciousness and interaction is small in comparison to the totality of the terrain. The total egg shape denotes the individual psyche or being. Ideally it should be seen as three dimensional, especially for its use in this interface area. The dotted line may then be seen to represent the boundary of the energy field, or aura, which is the term used esoterically to describe the energy which extends for between four to six inches out from the physical body. This aura can be seen clairvoyantly as light and colour.

The Lower Unconscious is the region of the being where unprocessed material is stored. It is the nature of the deep unconscious to be dark and undifferentiated rather in the way in which the negative of a photograph is undifferentiated. When this material begins to surface into consciousness it may seem shadowy and frightening. Deep dream content often contains coded messages from this part of the being. The psyche will have had good reasons for storing the things that are there in the Lower Unconscious at the time at which the storage happened, but as growth and development takes place those reasons may no longer be valid. With courage and support it is possible to release unconscious repressed emotions, and by so doing gain access to additional creative psychic energy. Holding things in the unconscious region takes effort; releasing them releases energy and often wisdom into the psyche.

* *See Glossary. Page 174.*

That which is kept repressed when it wants to surface can also gain a negative autonomy, and begin to govern the actions, thoughts and desires of the individual. Such autonomous forces are all too often mistaken for 'guidance', and discussion of this will continue throughout this book.

The Middle Unconscious is the region in which those things which are relatively easy to recall are stored. Here lies information not being directly held in consciousness, but which can be remembered or recalled at will. This includes skills which have been learned, like reading and writing, and which are reflexively, or relatively unconsciously used.

Often this material will have direct input into the standards or constructs around which life and expression revolve. The stuff of the Middle Unconscious may relate to things which happened or were thought about yesterday or last week, or to much earlier parts of life, but it is material which, relative to the Lower Unconscious content, has been accepted into the psyche or is in process of such acceptance. During the journey of conscious growth, that which inhabits the realm of the Middle Unconscious will be under constant revision.

The Higher Unconscious is the region which is of particular interest when considering the interface between the worlds of psychology and spiritual exploration. Here is the realm of potential, of peak experience, of higher intuition and aspiration. It is also a region which often needs to be fertilized by the compost of the Lower Unconscious before it becomes totally activated and accessible at will. Later in this book I shall super-impose upon the egg map, a chakra map, in order to demonstrate the importance of, and possibilities for choosing the area and the energies to be activated in the search for guidance.

The Field of Usual Consciousness is small in area in comparison to the total scope of the map. It contains that which is in our awareness and conscious interaction at any given moment in time. As you read this book you will be conscious of what you are reading, perhaps of the words on the page, and of thoughts, personal resonances, in relation to what you are reading. You may also be conscious, depending on your environment, of peripheral things either impinging on or enhancing your well being. As I write these words, I am concentrating on a train of thought, but am also aware of background music which I find an aid to concentration. I am using acquired typing skills. (Such reflexive skills or abilities are stored in the Middle Unconscious). The sound of the lawn mower outside is an impingement in one sense, but also speaks to me unmistakably of England in June. Into this Field of Usual Consciousness then, come the events, the skills and the reactions of the moment, the present, as they are required for normal functioning and interaction.

Psychologically speaking there is an implication that everything of which there is consciousness has to be brought into this Field. The material to be examined is moved into the area, rather than the Usual Field of Consciousness moving towards the material. In what is regarded as normal functioning and interaction I would accept and believe this to be true, but in the area of interface and moving into the spiritual dimension I would suggest that there is a subtle but important difference. In my experience of spiritual functioning, at a certain point, the Usual Field of Consciousness moves out into the territory, and the territory changes from the limitations of psychological terrain into other planes and spheres of consciousness, revealing further worlds of 'other reality', interpenetrating powerfully with that which is more ordinarily perceived as real.

I see this as a crucial area of interface containing un-limited potential as well as certain dangers. This moving out into other planes of awareness is related to what are often called 'altered states of consciousness'. I write 're-lated to', because there are degrees in altered states, and these degrees are the whole essence of the territory of interface. They are the reason for stating that psychologi-cal understanding must precede, and also go strongly alongside spiritual journeying if there is to be safety of passage between the interpenetrating worlds. Someone sensing this change during guided imagery, later described the experience thus:

'Suddenly what was in my consciousness was no longer merely appearing to me, I was aware that I was appearing to it, as well.' This sort of observation is invaluable in differentiating levels of guidance, and their lead into and relationship with discarnate guidance.

Outside the dotted line which denotes the boundary of the individual psyche, (i.e. the outer line of the egg map), lies the area which is called The Collective Unconscious. This is where there can be interaction with other people at those subtle levels which are powerful, and yet essentially unconscious until the facility for self observation and self consciousness is sharpened and extended. The dotted lines of the egg of the psyche in the map imply indeed, that 'no man is an island'. He is subject to infiltrations from the immediate environment, from atmospheres, from the moods of others, but more widely still from a racial consciousness, and eventually from the totality which is the Collective Unconscious. It is possible then to be open to and to have access to the sum total of all the experience of mankind, both positive and negative.

Those who are particularly sensitive or open in the mesh around the egg, may be regarded as, or feel themselves to be 'psychic'. Their response to collective events and to people in their environment may go beyond the accepted norm for sensitivity. They may be subject to premonitions, or dream vivid dreams. 'Feelings', about future, or current events, which prove to be accurate, may be part of their extended experience of life. There may be awareness of subtle energies and life forms, such as auras,* and elementals.*

In using the word, 'psychic', in a chapter which is also discussing interface, it must be noted that psychologically the word means:- 'of the psyche'. In spiritual and esoteric worlds it has come to mean the ability to be open in the way described above. Terms like 'psychic strength', or 'psychic boundaries' will not necessarily mean the same to the psychologist as they would to the spiritual seeker. This Collective area around the individual psyche, is the space in which we all live and move and have our being. It is also, according to the plane of functioning, at any given moment, the place of the interpenetration of spiritual and psychic realms, and of discarnate entities. My contact with Gildas is by shift of consciousness which allows me to be

See Glossary.

more open to the dimension where he functions or has being, and which enables him to approach clearly and closely into my awareness. Often, but not always, the contact will have that quality of closeness, that clarity of 'level shift' which brings the experience already mentioned, of *movement* of my Usual Field of Consciousness onto, or into his plane or dimension.

The particular interface areas now under discussion are important ones in clarifying the boundaries between Psychology, and Esoteric Spiritual Exploration. The main concern of Psychology is with the present personality, and how it has reacted to the environmental stimuli of this life. It is concerned with the study of human behaviour, and its positive and negative modifications. Transpersonal Psychology moves into consideration of spiritual purpose and drives, setting the life into spiritual context. Most Transpersonal Psychologists will work with a sense of 'higher self', 'higher will', or perhaps 'soul', encouraging contact with such a level to help forward the understanding which goes alongside awareness, growth, and positive change. There is a wide acceptance now in the study of human behaviour and potential that there are 'altered states' of consciousness, and therefore different levels of perception, different levels of experiencing 'reality'.

The concept of the Collective Unconscious is one of the tenets of Jungian Psychology. In the last paragraph I move through these areas of interface into a different realm when I speak, not of levels of consciousness or awareness, but of planes of functioning or being, and introduce the concepts of discarnate beings and guides. The *discarnate state* implies that there is a continuance of life beyond the physical 'here and now'. This is a spiritual, metaphysical and religious concept which may have to be taken into account in psychological investigation of human behaviour, but which is beyond the scope of pure psychological premise or hypothesis.

In and through my personal understanding of the discarnate state is a belief in, and acceptance of reincarnation and many lifetimes. These beliefs colour my personal understanding and definition of the Collective Unconscious and lead me to the statement: 'According to the plane on which we are functioning'. What needs to be clear is that the acceptance of the Collective Unconscious is not always synchronous with the acceptance of other planes of being and functioning, just as belief in the discarnate state and the continuance of life beyond physical death is not necessarily synchronous with belief in reincarnation and many lifetimes.

It is my conviction that the search for guidance must be accompanied by personal psychological exploration, with the objective of self-knowledge, and gaining psychological transparency in regard to projections, identifications, and conditioned prejudices. Clear inner guidance often develops during, and as a result of such exploration. If the aim is to cross the interface into the contact with discarnate guidance, then the discrimination necessary to the safe exploration and interpretation of other worlds and planes is only gained through psychological self knowledge. Where projections and unrecognised but powerful sub-personalities have a degree of autonomy within the psyche, any level of guidance which is contacted may be coloured by drive, control, and limiting or rigid authoritarianism. There will always be a degree of 'colouring' in guidance, but in my experience the key notes of the true guides, both inner, (from the transpersonal psychological levels), and discarnate, are unconditional love, or positive regard; acceptance; gentle humour; and deep wisdom without drive or threat.

Consideration of these points will continue, alongside the exercises in this book aimed to give greater understanding of, and access to subtle sensitivities. This understanding comes with movement from the map into the territory. There is one more feature of this map of the psyche to discuss however before moving on to exploration of sensitivity.

The points on the diagram, which are numbered '6', and here called the Transpersonal, or Sun Self, have relevance to potential, and becoming, and also to inner guidance. As self-knowledge and insight develop, so glimpses of the fully empowered being are also released. If anyone was functioning totally from the Transpersonal or Sun Self, all the time, the learning process of life would probably be finished. In deepest and highest moments of consciousness comes the acquaintance with this aspect of being. At first, before the search begins, functioning and perception will largely be confined to the ego self, *(5)* and its interpretation of events. As growth progresses, the wisdom of more total experience brings contact with this higher aspect. It is mapped as being in an area of interface, a place where there is access to other perspectives. In the original egg map of Assagioli, it appeared always, and only at the top of the map. It is accessible if it is allowed to be, to all areas of the psyche, and therefore in the diagram given here is mapped all around the egg, not because it is necessarily conceived as multiple, but to denote its accessibility. Jung spoke of the self, (with small 's'), and the Self, (with capital 'S'); Maslow of Self-Realization, and Self-Actualization. Again terms are not completely interchangeable, and rather less so when speaking spiritually of the Higher Self. There are correspondences and similarities, which do not cancel each other out, but rather enrich the frame of reference for understanding. These terms will be used many times, and in context I hope they will aid clarity. An exciting aspect of the acceptance of interface is that once such areas are recognized, the exploration is under way. Like the air lock area in spacecraft there is enablement for leaving one area in order to enter another, and also enablement for return. There is interface all around us. When recognized it aids communication, the extending of boundaries of perception, freedom from rigidity, and the constant raising of the ceiling of human potential.

How then, to conduct the business of inner exploration, the search for guidance and greater clarity as to the levels of the being? In workshops I give which form a series, the first workshop is entitled: 'Exploring Sensitivity'. It is my belief that many people have greater sensitivity towards others, towards the environment, and towards themselves than they allow into conscious realization. Sometimes the complaint, 'I cannot visualize', is based on an expectation about visualization which proves to be a limitation. In perceiving the world around us there is a tendency to describe that perception in terms of the physical senses of sight, taste, touch, hearing and smell, and to link sensory experience to the organs associated with these five senses. The things that can be perceived in these ways we call 'real', thus the outer tangible, material world tends to hold all the power of that reality, and to become the model for perception. Inner perceptions become identified with 'imagination', which instead of being seen as another reality in its own right, is often deemed to be in opposition to reality. In inner and spiritual exploration different areas, realms and levels of perception will occur. If there is to be benefit from these experiences, then such perception must be seen as other dimensions of reality. Different realities, but having relationship and interface with the accepted and objective world of physical reality. In the same way if the expected mode of perception stays too linked to the physical senses and organs of perception, there will be constant disappointment in inner eyes which do not see, inner ears which do not hear and so on.

The business of exploration is that of pushing against boundaries and limited expectations, into territories where imagination is an instrument of perception, where sensing and sensitivity are extensions and combinations of the experience of physical perception, and where subjective involvement brings new definitions of that which is 'real'. In exploration it is also necessary to develop the quality of self observation. Do not then *expect* inner perceptions to be as outer perceptions. Be expectant, but with an open expectancy. Be flexible, ready to observe how inner perception does communicate itself to your consciousness. Be open to perceptions which are a 'knowing', needing perhaps more physically sensate terminology for purposes of interpretation or communication. Paradoxically it must also be said here that many people do experience the inner worlds with almost direct physically sensate connection. At this point they are probably wondering when description of the exercises is to begin!

In a workshop group, the introduction will be of necessity somewhat cerebral and Left Brain orientated. (At a certain point in the physical brain, there are two distinct 'hemispheres'. The left brain hemisphere governs language, logical thought communication, conceptualization etc. The right brain hemisphere is more related to the world of phantasy, intuition, artistic and imaginative creativity.) Switching to something which is more Right Brain orientated can be a great help in stretching the normal boundaries of perception.

Fairly soon then, I ask the group to find partners, (usually someone they do not know well), and to endeavour to perceive, or receive that person, *sense* that person, in terms of an animal, a colour, and a fragrance. It must be clear that this exercise is *not* a telepathic exercise. The person who is being sensed must be as passive as possible, not trying to transmit any of these things to the person who is doing the sensing. Later in the day a similar exercise is done as a telepathic exercise, in order to demonstrate the different energy, between sensing or receiving another person in this way, and endeavouring to pick up a specific message which is being transmitted.

When partners have been selected, and the decision has been made about who is to be completely passive and who is to do the 'sensing', those who are to be active, decide on how best to receive the impressions of their partner. Usually the eyes are closed, and there is a deep quality of concentration and receptivity. Some people hold hands, others use their hands as 'sensors' running gently around the energy field, or auric field of the person they are working with, yet others put their hands on their partner's shoulders. In a few moments, the images, or the information, in the specific form in which it is asked for is there. The partner who has been active, then tells the 'passive' partner which animal, colour and fragrance has been perceived. Usually there is a meaningful recognition of these perceptions. The 'active' participant may have had a compelling sense of a black cat, for instance, and the partner reveals a strong feeling for a black cat, or has dreamed of one the night before.

These correspondences, are so consistent throughout the group, as to be startling or exciting, the more so because usually there is little expectation at this stage from the exercise, and I sometimes get the impression at the beginning, that people are participating in order to humour *me!* Where there is no reaction or correspondence from the one who has been sensed, in discussion it may emerge that what has been found is of strong significance to someone else working nearby, or that the active partner has surfaced something for himself/herself which was barely conscious, and suddenly takes on meaningful association. Whatever happens the resulting discussion makes the group, and the individuals who form that group keen to observe processes, to discuss, and to open up to possibilities. Everyone gets a turn to be active, and to be passive, but partners are changed after the first round, because pure telepathic contact is being directly avoided at this stage.

My recommendation in the group situation is that the partners should not know each other well, that friends who have come to the group together separate for this exercise. This is because correspondences are so much more dramatic and notable when people may not have met before. Working at home though, the exercise can be used with a cooperative friend, since it provides an opening for discussion, for a different way of perception, and even with someone well known unexpected correspondences can occur. Perhaps the most important aspect of this exercise is that it gives material for observation and discussion, and begins to awaken the all important aspect of 'the observer', or capacity for self observation in the field of perception. In these times there is easy talk about 'extra-sensory perception', without perhaps sufficient thought about what those words actually mean. Extra-sensory perception is not only related to the worlds of mediumship or telepathy. Most of us are making perceptions which go beyond the normal or conscious use of the senses all the time. Sometimes there is not enough pause for observation or analysis of the complexities of perception, or of the different ways in which the information on which we form opinions and judgements is coming towards us.

The next area which is given attention in a workshop on 'Exploring Sensitivity', *is* the area of the physical senses. It is not often that there is opportunity to differentiate these, and concentrate on them specifically one at a time. Having begun to establish that perception often goes beyond the physical senses, concentrating on each one in turn can bring insights, and help in the process of widening the model of reference. For the purpose of the exercise, not five, but six senses are explored, the sixth one being a very physical one, the kinesthetic sense. This is the sense of being conscious of the body in its movements, and really focussing into its action.

Most people like to 'lie out', for this exploration, on the floor, with a rug for warmth, and a pillow for comfort. In the workshop situation the exercise carries on from sense to sense, with a short pause between each one for the jotting of notes. If you are attempting this observation at home, I suggest that you spread it over several days, and allow time for staying more conscious of the way in which a particular sense operates for you in daily life. The structure of the exercise, and going too quickly from sense to sense, and stage to stage could bring about an altered state of consciousness. Leading the procedure in a workshop, I am able to monitor the pace, and watch reactions in individuals. If you are not used to handling altered states of consciousness, and particularly if you are working alone, I hope you will heed the advice to go gradually, and to consider one sense thoroughly before passing to the next.

Each sense is explored in three stages, two minutes allowed for each stage. The first stage focusses the particular sense chosen, into the immediate environment. Thus, working with the sense of sight, participants are asked to look around the room, and to notice whatever objects draw their attention. It is difficult to look at something without forming a judgement about it, e.g. 'That's beautiful', 'too brightly coloured', 'very old', etc. but part of the discipline of this exercise is just to observe, without judgement, whilst being aware of how difficult it is to do that. The next stage is with eyes closed, and four different things are given for visualization. These are a random selection, but usually include a seascape.

A typical instruction might be: Close your eyes: Visualize: . . . a favourite seascape . . .; the geometric shape of a green triangle . . .; the face of someone you love . . . ; a room you know well . . .

The final stage is instructed thus: *Keeping your eyes closed, get a sense of going more deeply into your personal inner space, sink into it, or stretch out towards it, and allow yourself to see whatever is there to be seen. . .*

At this point time is allowed for noting any comments about the experience, but not yet for discussion. Before going on to consider the observations which I encourage people to draw out from this exercise, I will give the rest of the procedure in full. If you want to use this, a good way of doing so is to put the instructions on tape for yourself, leaving the appropriate pauses. This can help with timing when working alone. If working with a friend you can either read the instructions for each other, or put them on tape and enter the experience together. I repeat, though, that *out* of the group situation, it is preferable to deal with one sense at a time, leaving a considerable gap before embarking on the next.

The order of working with the senses is not important, but I usually put another sense between taste and smell since these two are very related. The next area for observation then may be the sense of touch . . .

Lie down and relax, or sit somewhere where you can be at ease. You can have your eyes open or closed, but know that you are concentrating on the sense of touch, as it applies to your immediate and present contact with the physical environment. With your fingers, touch things which are in reach, feel the texture of them, be aware of your fingers moving over different surfaces. Remember that the whole body experiences touch, so be aware of the chair or the floor touching your body, be aware of the contact of your clothes with your body, the air coming from your nostrils, your tongue in your mouth . . .

Now close your eyes, and feel the texture of the bark of a tree . . .; feel the warm texture of wet sand . . .; stroke a warm animal . . .; hold an ice cube . . .

Get that sense now, of going more deeply into your personal inner space, move towards it or into it, and experience the touch of anything which is there to be touched . . .

The next move is to the sense of smell:

Again, begin by making sure that you are relaxed; you are now focussing on the sense of smell; first of all, either with your eyes open, or closed, whichever seems most appropriate or comfortable, concentrate on the immediate physical environment, and anything in that environment which you perceive through your sense of smell . . . if you have had your eyes open to begin with, close them, or vice versa, and observe whether there is any difference of perception for your sense of smell . . .

Now, with your eyes closed, go within: . . . and smell the smell of wood smoke . . . ; smell the tang of a place by the sea . . . ; smell hot tar . . . ; smell the fragrance of a rose . . .

Go further now into your inner space, get a sense of taking a deeper or further step within, and smell whatever is there to be smelled . . .

31

After a suitable time, move to the sense of hearing:

Relax again, and focus on your sense of hearing as it applies to your immediate and present environment . . . listen to the sounds which you can physically hear, now; again, experiment with eyes open and eyes closed, but stay with the physical surroundings . . .

Close your eyes now, if you have not already done so. Go within; hear the sound of distant church bells . . . ; hear a clock ticking in a quiet room . . . ; hear someone's voice calling your name . . . ; listen to the sound of the sea . . .

Enter again that deeper inner space, relax into it, and hear or listen to the sounds which are there to be heard . . .

When it feels right to do so, prepare to observe in like manner your sense of taste:

Be relaxed, and begin to explore your present sense of physical taste, being aware of the mechanism of taste, the function and movement of your tongue in your mouth; endeavour to experience the taste of your present environment . . .

Close your eyes and go within: taste the taste of fresh lemon . . . ; hot cabbage . . . ; strawberry ice-cream . . . the tang of the sea . . .

Go more fully into your inner space, entering positively a deeper place in your being, and experience any taste which is there . . .

The final sense for exploration, when you are ready, is the kinesthetic sense, previously mentioned. In this exploration you focus into your body, not just in a tactile sense, but by feeling yourself into a fuller consciousness of its movement, and mechanisms.

Starting once again from a comfortable position, first of all, get in touch with your body, and how it is arranged and distributed in physical space, at this moment; then move your body, your limbs, your head, feet, fingers, . . . be conscious of the part which is moving, and all the sensation of movement; vary the pace and the sense of lightness or heaviness in your movement, during this experience . . .

Take up an easy position again, and close your eyes; in the first stage of inner space which has been established during this total exploration of the senses, experience your bodily movement: as you ride a bicycle up an incline with the wind against you . . . ; ,12as you search for a piece of slippery soap in the bath . . . ; as you run on firm wet sand . . . ; as you lie relaxed in a warm natural environment . . .

Go to the deeper level of inner space, and be aware of how you sense and realize yourself there; move in that space, and feel into your quality of movement in that space as you do so . . .

As you finish each section, make at least some outline notes, of your self observation process. Reflect on these and on some of the implications and further potential which this investigation holds. In a workshop situation, as the whole exercise comes to an end, groups for discussion are formed, and experiences and observations are compared.

At this stage, not everybody will have been able to experience the two suggested levels of inner space. This is natural; with practise, and relaxation, greater confidence and sharpened discriminatory faculties, it will come. Equally, some people have difficulty with the first stage of inner space, but feel free, released and joyful in the second stage. The important thing to re-member is that an investigation like this is not a test. It is a means of better self knowledge, of cultivat-ing the 'observer', and of seeing potential for further self-training.

Before the groups in a workshop begin their discussion and sharing, I suggest certain points to which considera-tion might be given, questions to ask oneself, and others. To what degree can you stay with one sense before others come in? If you are endeavouring to hear church bells in the distance, are you actually able to hear the sound before visualization of a scene comes in? Or, do you need the scene in order to get in touch with the sound? When working with the first inner stage of the senses, can you evaluate how far your experience is based on remember-ing, and how far you were able to bring the suggested experience into the present moment? If you are not a good 'visualizer', is there any other sense which is stronger for you, and might therefore 'lead', as you endeavour to create and discover more of your inner worlds, and the inner planes?

If you find it difficult, (as most people do), to isolate the sense you are working with, so that, for example before you can feel the texture of the bark of a tree you have to visualize the whole tree, or even an entire forest of trees, practise with these exercises can bring a greater sense of precision, and definition. It is not necessary to become *over* analytical, but in many ways, as one opens to exploration of sensitivity, and breadth of experience it is desirable to discover as a child discovers, by building up experience, by testing it out, and noting that which is constant and that which is variable; those skills which have been mastered, and those which need more attention.

Often there are unexpected bonuses discovered during the course of this particular exercise. Someone who is hard of hearing in the physical world rediscovered the joy of remembered sounds stored in the 'inner ear', and the clarity of sound in that deeper level of inner space. Someone suffering loss of smell, rediscovered its delights in these inner places, and subsequently reported improvement in 'outer' smell.

A sense such as smell is often enormously evocative, and particularly in this section of the exploration, specific memories or incidents in life may be evoked. In considering the total response to the exercise, another thing to note and perhaps to investigate further is the nature of any memories which may have emerged, and why they may have 'spoken' from the psyche at this particular time.

The theme of the sea is included in each of the senses, to facilitate comparison, and the investigation of the question, 'Which is my leading sense?'

The visualizing of the 'face of someone you love', is often surprisingly difficult. This is included to illustrate the point that perception is extremely complex. Those close to us, we experience deeply as the precious and intricate beings they are. We remember their essence and completeness much more easily than their face or physical appearance.

I have said enough to show that there is much to be drawn out of this exercise. It repays repetition, and serves as a point of discipline for differentiating the senses. It gives a creative departure point for defining different areas or depths of inner space, and as a basis for comparing inner sensing experience with outer sensing experience.

Once the quest of exploring sensitivity has begun, and attention given to one's perceptions, sustainment of that attention will bring response from the psyche in terms of gradual expansion and sharpening of sensitive awareness. Since it is easy to lose sight of progress, to the extent that when a new place is reached, the place from which the journey began is often forgotten, I do recommend that you keep some sort of record, or journal of comments, observations and feelings. Look back to the beginning from time to time and evaluate any development or enrichment.

After the rather long exercise and discussion on the senses, in a workshop, a rounding off is made by attempting to experience the energies of telepathy, in contrast to the energies of sensing, which were highlighted in the first interaction, concerned with the animal, the fragrance, and the colour. Often it is only through attempting to enter an experience, that true understanding of subtle differences in the energies of perception can come. In a group situation it is impossible to set up the sort of scientific and objective conditions which are necessary to a study of telepathy. In this interaction, then, no 'test' is implied, no really objective conclusions can be drawn, but in a group of co-operative individuals, certain coincidences, and synchroncities, which appear to go beyond the laws of chance can usually be observed.

The experience is organised in a similar way to the first exercise. Partners are selected, and a decision taken as to who shall begin as 'transmitter', and who as 'receiver'. Since fragrance is rather a diffuse and individual awareness, and therefore not easy to transmit, the task now, is to send to the receiving partner, by concentration and transmission, a flower, an animal or bird, and a colour. In this exercise neither partner is completely passive, the transmitter endeavours to send a clear image or message, and the receiver becomes as receptive as possible to that transmission.

Using telepathic energy, it is often easier to transmit or to receive a word rather than an image, and this needs to be discussed by the partners. It is also known from studies of telepathic potential, that some people are better transmitters, and others better receivers. In the workshop, the partner selection is completely random. Two people with receptive ability, or two people with transmitting ability working together may get little result at this stage. Yet when the moment comes to investigate the experience in the group as a whole, the individual partnership results take on a different significance.

In this exploration, since there is now an endeavour to build up a link and an extra sensory communication between two people, partners are not changed, to give everyone the experience of transmission and reception, the roles are merely reversed. Each object is transmitted separately, and the receiving partner is given the information: '*I am now concentrating on and transmitting a flower . . . (colour; . . . animal/bird).*'

A common difficulty experienced, is for the receiver, in staying with the first impression received. The mind is split-second quick to superimpose something which seems more logical or reasonable. Often when a transmitter says that what has been received as a horse, started out as an eagle, the receiver will recall a momentary impression of powerful wings, or height, or a talon, which was then rejected. How many times in life is immediate clarity of impression overriden by logic or reason? The *interaction* of logic and reason with any level of perception is to be desired, but this exercise often serves to demonstrate how quickly the opportunity for this interaction can be blocked, because the intuitive or 'hunch' aspect is overlooked or undervalued. This illuminates once again a point to watch in self-development: the isolation and identification of *each stage* in the process by which judgements and hence commitments are made.

The stage of looking at what has happened in the group during this exercise is usually an interesting one. I make a list of all the colours, flowers, animals and birds which have been transmitted, and all those which have been received. As this is made there are usually exclamations that a pink flamingo transmitted from one side of the room has been received instead of a fox, on the other side of the room, and perhaps vice versa. I have not yet done any real research into my experience of this exercise with groups, but the number of things which have been received without having been transmitted *anywhere* in the room is usually remarkably low, and especially so in a residential workshop, or where the group has worked together before. The things which have been transmitted are also often remarkably limited, considering the width of selection available, and there will be frequent repetitions of the most unusual animals or flowers. All this seems to indicate that individuals in a group intent on helping each other to experience other levels of communication and perception, become more sensitively attuned than is the norm. This sensitivity is a group, as well as an individual experience.

In this chapter, I have moved from the chosen map of the psyche, through an initial discussion on interface, into the beginnings of the exploration of the individual territory. In the following chapter, as I lead in to more specific comments about Guidance, the theme moves from the general map of the psyche, into the personal mapping and experiencing of inner territory and dimensions. First, let this present section end on a lighter note. In the workshop groups, once people relax, there is always a lot of laughter. I have previously mentioned the comparison of exploring the field and the language of inner worlds as a child explores, with openness. I also recommend a sense of play. The play world of the child, is the means of his or her investigation and assimilation of the environment. There is a growing structuring and consciousness in the phantasy and experimentation. So it must be for ourselves, at least in part, if the language and 'rules' of inner space are not only to be observed and perceived, but also an integral and valued expansion of daily life. Recapture then, the joy of play. Delight in that reality which is imagination, and though serious in the quest, do not forget the value of laughter, adding a lightness of touch, and an energy to the journey.

CHAPTER 2

The Inner Dimension: Charting the Territory.

The Assagioli Egg Map of the Psyche which is under discussion, is an attempt to map the human psyche in general terms. When making a journey in the physical world, a map or an atlas may be consulted to give a sense of dimension and proportion. There may be movement from a large route planning map, to a more detailed road map, or ordnance survey map. In the province of the psyche particularly in the transpersonal and spiritual regions the only maps, (such as the Egg Map) are in the nature of the general atlas or route planner. The inner territory is personal and specific. From the point of the general map onwards, this personal territory can only be mapped by the individual through conscious experience. In the physical world, a whole group may take the same route using maps which are very detailed, even pictorial, using reassuring landmarks for recognition. At the total personal experiential level each individual in the group will make a different journey, will see different perspectives, find different aspects the most worthy of note, and have different reactions. Photographs or descriptions, or drawings of the scenery will, however be commonly recognized. The whole group will be able to say,

'Oh, that is the hotel at . . . '.

In the inner worlds, each territory, each journey, even though it is a 'guided journey' will be different. Each will be experienced differently and expressed differently. There will be an individual significance which relates particularly to the psychological life patterns and the constructs, freedoms, blockages and tenets which arise from these.

Although each individual journey is different, it is still possible to take quite a large group on a 'guided journey', and to give instructions to the group about certain inner landmarks which may be met with and experienced. After the journey, it will be found that most of the group has had some encounter with the suggested symbols.

There is collective, and therefore to some extent objective agreement and acceptance surrounding such symbols as 'The Tree of Life'. It is there in most inner territories, but in drawing, description etc. there is no common or objective representation of that which each or everyone will have known in personal inner space. For some The Tree of Life may be a mighty oak, for others a graceful willow. Yet others may find it stunted or blasted or they will draw on better known representations such as the Kabbalistic, or Alchemical Tree of Life.

The actual territory then, is subjective. The form of the experienced objects often gives important messages for self development. There is also a shared response, and in discussing the individual journeys, interpersonal and intrapersonal communication deepen.

In physical territory once a journey has been made, it can be repeated. Depending on the complexity of the travel the repeat may or may not be accompanied by a map of the territory. A daily journey soon requires no map though the route may change a little due to the discovery of a 'short cut' or scenic detour. Many people who have experience of the inner worlds come across a particular aspect of the territory by chance or by experiencing a piece at a time. The return to a particular part can neither be reliably calculated, mapped or expected, or so it feels. One of my concerns in working with individuals and groups is to rectify this, and through the building up of inner experience, help the inner landscape to become as familiar and knowable as outer territory. In the analogy I have used of a daily journey in the outer world, familiarity with the route brings the courage to attempt a diversion, or to explore a little further. I believe the same to be true of the inner worlds. Structured exploration together with personal familiarity and 'mapping' builds up the confidence to go further and to use the inner landscape as a source of strength, wisdom and guidance.

Symbols such as the Tree of Life are archetypal symbols, or, in the words of The Oxford Dictionary: 'primordial mental image(s) inherited by all'. There are many such symbols in the inner worlds, and figures too. By seeking them in the four elements, in a guided imagery type journey, a first personal mapping of inner space can be made. Objects and types of terrain are sought first; seeking and meeting with figures, later, begins to establish insight into levels of guidance.

The building up, or exploration of inner space in this way can result in pictures resembling something akin to John Bunyan's 'A Pilgrim's Progress', with the 'Slough of Despond', the 'Lions on the Path', or 'The Gate Beautiful'. The journey and the landscape are thus allegorical. The journey of Christian represents a spiritual pilgrimage of a particular historical time and idiom. Each individual experiencing inner world reality enters into an allegorical and symbolic journey of self-understanding. It is the allegory of the personal mental, emotional, physical and spiritual journey through incarnation. It reflects and informs the search for that understanding which gives a fuller sense of the ability to embrace the mysteries and apparent inconsistencies of life itself.

The first part of the exploration is like taking an aerial view of the inner landscape, in order to get an overall sense of content and what the potentials and weaknesses may be. It is necessary to maintain a certain level of detachment at this stage. In later exercises the symbols and happenings in the inner landscape need more interpretation and are probably more interpretable, but at this stage it is important to be the observer, to have the feeling of building up knowledge which will help other stages of the inner journey.

To help to achieve this level of detachment the first part of this enquiry is entitled 'The Magic Carpet' exercise. It is seen as a four part journey or exploration, each part emphasizing a particular element. The element which is under exploration determines the basic archetypal symbols or aspects of the inner landscape to be noted or marked. In between each element it is helpful to have a large sheet of paper and crayons or paints for the recording of the journey.

Drawing and painting are very helpful media for the recording of inner explorations. Many people feel inhibited at first about their drawing ability, but it can literally be 'matchstick' or symbolic drawing, as equally it can be fully artistic and expansive work. Drawing, being more related to right brain activity than to the logical, sequential recording of the left brain, helps the energy of intuition and heart to flow, and the inner territory thus to reveal its riches and its secrets.

If you feel *really* inhibited by drawing then a written record is of course acceptable, but if you can develop even minimal drawing and colour, it will be a helpful and integral part of the experience. I speak here from personal empathy. My drawing ability is minimal, and is further limited by eyesight which makes perspective and dimension difficult. At first then, I had great resistance to drawing as a recording medium, but gradually I have come to value it as an instant point of reference, which though primitive, is usually far more powerful and immediate than any written words can be. I usually write as well, and the one record enhances the other, but drawing has become for me a very essential ingredient to the connection between the inner exploration and the outer remembering, interpretation and communication.

To begin then, the 'Magic Carpet Exercise' of the four elements, make sure you have some undisturbed time and space and put some large paper and paint or crayons to hand. Before you begin know that you are going to take an aerial view of your inner territory in four sections. Between each section make a pause for recording, so that you do not build up too much material to retain with your head, intellect or mind. Read through the lists of symbolic objects and areas which you may encounter in each element, but feel completely free to reject some suggestions or to add others. Remember that certain aspects of the structure of the exercise *can* only be suggestions, your territory is personal to you, some of these things may be present now, some may appear later, and other things not listed or mentioned may be pertinent to you at this moment. Be open to your territory as it is, and use the suggestions as guidelines, not as rigid form.

In an inner journey or exploration it is helpful to be accompanied by a 'Talisman'. This is an object or symbol which ensures safety and which carries with it the ability to help at any moment when an energy access or change may be appropriate. You may already possess such a symbol or object in the outer world. Many people have rings, stones, or other 'amulets' which incorporate the power of the talisman for positive energization. In the inner world the talisman may be a live animal, or a symbol of a live animal, a plant, a jewel or a light of some description. In the first part of the journey the instructions include calling on the accompanying talisman for the journey. Thus you may restate your connection with something well known, establish your talisman for the first time, or take a well known talisman plus an extra talisman appropriate to this particular journey.

A personal talisman of mine is a snake, who sometimes accompanies me in 'live' form, sometimes symbolically as a bangle or carving on a stick or staff. If when you first ask for the accompaniment of a talisman none appears, make a mental selection of something which is meaningful for you and transfer it firmly into your inner space. A light, a jewel, a cross of light in a circle of light and so on.

The elements are explored in the order of a) Earth; b) Water; c) Air; d) Fire. To some extent they overlap, and are essential to each other, but endeavour to concentrate on one whilst being aware of where others may fit in, or interact.

In the element of *Earth* you will be noting the possibility of the presence of: the Mountain; the Forest; the Fertile Plain; the Arid Desert; the Marsh or Bog; the Island, the Sheltering Cave; the Pleasant Path; the Tree of Life; the Rocky Path; the Pit.

In the element of *Water* you will perhaps or probably encounter: the River of Life; the Source or Spring; the Sea, and/or Lake; the Waters of Peace; the Rapids; the Whirpool; the Icy Place, the Underground Stream.

In the element of *Air:* the Whirlwind; the Area of Low Pressure; the Place where it is Easy to Breathe; the Resting Place with Cooling Breeze; the Place where the Sun always Shines; the Mountain Top.

In the element of *Fire:* the Volcano; the Living Fire; the Hot Springs; the Lighthouse.

Some of these things may be one and the same: the Living Fire, may be in the Sheltering Cave, the Mountain Top may be the Place where the Sun always shines, etc. Some of the symbols in the way in which they are described take on a positive aspect, some a more negative aspect. Acceptance that this is so helps further work and exploration, and in bringing that which is still unconscious into consciousness.

If you are apprehensive about the thought of flying over your inner landscape on a magic carpet, decide on some other way, by which you gain an overall impression of the territory, for example, by climbing the mountain. If you are really hesitant about being too closely participant you can see your inner territory as though on a film or television screen, but the more you can participate the more open do these other levels of reality become. Never force anything, and always seek help, as suggested in the introduction to this book if you are hesitant or concerned about any aspect.

Before you begin, you may like to record the instructions for this guided journey, on a tape. Again doing this sort of exercise with a friend or small group is good, as there is then opportunity to compare reactions, experiences and imagery. To help you to record, or to lead yourself or others into this journey, I set it out below as given in workshops.

Make yourself comfortable, either in a meditative position, or lying down with a rug, and a pillow or cushion. Have your body symmetrically arranged, and supported where it may need support.

Become conscious of your breathing, and let the rhythm be gentle and easy. Sense each in-breath, and each out-breath in your heart centre. (That is, in the centre of your body, on a level with your physical heart.)

As you centre into this rhythm find yourself in a meadow, and in this meadow let your inner senses open, so that you see the colours; hear the sounds; smell the fragrances; know the textures; and taste the tastes. It may be a meadow you know, or one you have experienced in your inner world before; you may get a sense of building the images up consciously, or this meadow may just be immediately there for you. Know that this is a place to which you can return at any time, from any stage of the experience; that it is the starting place and the ending place for inner journeyings.

When you are fully into your meadow, ask if there is a talisman present with you to take on this journey; it may be a talisman you already know, or there may be some other one specially for you to take with you now.

There is also a magic carpet in the meadow, and you are going to fly on the magic carpet over your inner landscape. Because the carpet is a magic one, you have full thought control over it, so that it will always fly at the height and speed you choose and will return you gently to the meadow at any time you wish it to do so.

The exploration of your inner territory is in four parts, concentrating on a consciousness of the four elements. The first element to explore is the element of Earth. As the elements interact and are necessary to each other, you may also be aware in the element of Earth, of the presence of Water, Fire or Air but in this first stage focus on the physical layout of the terrain.

Get onto your magic carpet and travel now to take an over all view of the landscape. Remember that in the element of earth you may find: the Mountain; the Forest; the Fertile Plain; the Arid Desert; the Marsh or Bog; the Island; the Sheltering Cave; the Pleasant Path; the Tree of Life; the Rocky Path; the Pit. . . . Any or all of these things, along with others specifically or personally meaningful to you may be present in your landscape. . . . Spend five minutes viewing all these possibilities from your magic carpet, then return to the meadow; leave your magic carpet there; return to the environment in which you are in physical reality, take your paper and crayons or paints, and begin to sketch out, or in some way to record the impressions you have received at this first stage of the exploration. Work quickly at your drawing, you can elaborate it later if you wish. Take not more than ten minutes to record this first general impression . . .

Now centre yourself again, breathing in your heart centre as before, and prepare to explore the element of Water in your inner landscape. Go to your meadow, reconnect with your talisman and your magic carpet, and take again a journey over this inner territory, knowing that in the element of Water you may find: the River of Life; the Source or Spring; the Sea, and/or Lake; the Waters of Peace; the Rapids; the Whirlpool; the Icy Place; the Underground Stream; . . . any or all of these as well as others pertinent to your own experience may be present for you now in the element of Water. Spend five minutes exploring the element of Water from your magic carpet, and then return again to the meadow; leave your magic carpet there, return to your outer physical environment, and spend between five to ten minutes adding the element of Water to your record of this journey. . . .

Use your breath in your heart chakra to help you to centre once more. Go again to your meadow, your talisman, and your magic carpet. You are now going to explore the element of Air in your inner landscape. . . . In the element of Air you may find: the Whirlwind; the Area of Low Pressure; the Place where it is Easy to Breathe; the Resting Place with Cooling Breeze; the Place where the Sun always Shines; the Mountain Top. Spend five minutes exploring the element of Air from your magic carpet, before returning again to the meadow, to your outer environment, and to your drawing or recording. At this stage five minutes should suffice in which to add the element of Air to your picture. . . .

For the final time re-centre yourself, feel your breath in your heart chakra, and return to the meadow, your talisman and your magic carpet, to prepare for the exploration of the element of Fire. In the element of Fire you may find: the Volcano; the Living Fire; the Hot Springs; the Light House - any or all of these, and other things of the Fire element which may be present for you personally and specifically in your inner landscape at this time. . . . Spend five minutes exploring the Fire element in your inner landscape, then come back to the meadow, take final leave of your magic carpet, and return to your present outer environment. Feel your feet firmly in contact with the ground, be aware of your whole body, and focus right into the outer world again. You can now add the Fire element to your drawing and also elaborate other aspects of it if you wish. Before you break off completely to go about other tasks, give some attention to your heart centre, visualizing that the petals* of the heart chakra are gently folded in, and flexible, so that you are not too open as you go about your ordinary business. . . .

If you are working at home or with a friend or small group, this exploration could, of course cover more than one session. You will probably find that you want to spend some time after its completion with your drawing or notebook. Many people completely re-draw their landscape, treating the quick work done during the exercise as a 'sketch notebook'.

This initial overview of the inner landscape, means that there is now a reference grid of this other reality which can become increasingly meaningful and more closely experi-

---

* *See Page 100 and glossary for fuller description of the chakras.*

ential. Part of this meaningfulness is that the inner reality gives a valuable tool for understanding one's life, for healing aspects of life experience, and for differentiating guidance patterns which are almost always already present.

The next stage in the exploration then, is to take an overview of the actual physical, mental and emotional journey through life. Doing this should bring further insight into the personal dynamic of the Assagiolo Egg Map of the Psyche. In order to help make links with the Magic Carpet journey and to prepare to release some of the healing potential of that exercise, I refer again to the diagrams on Page 19. On Page 47. a cross has been superimposed on the egg diagram. The horizontal line of the cross goes through the area designated in the egg diagram as the Middle Unconscious. The vertical line crosses all the areas of the psyche, from the depths of the Lower Unsonscious, through the ego centre, to connect with Assagioli's original placing of the Sun Self at the top of the egg.

Personal experience of the significance of the dynamic of this cross, in terms of the journey through life came to me about three years ago when I spent an extended time meditating in Chartres Cathedral. In a barefoot walking meditation, I felt identified with the Psyche of the Cathedral itself, yet contained within it. As I walked from North to South images from my actual physical and emotional life came to me. Standing at the central point of this axis, I looked back on my birth into this incarnation, and forward to my death. There was a calmness and a detachment within me, but from this perspective, I was aware of questions as to meaning and purpose, but of a basic limitation in normal ego consciousness.

I commenced a similar walking journey from West to East. As I stood at the West door looking towards the East, I was aware of power and purpose, and essence of Spirit coming from the traditional direction of all that is Holy. As I walked towards the West, the vision of the egg diagram came to me, as I have now drawn it on Page 47. The journey of body, mentality and emotions, had resulted in considerable material being relegated to the Lower Unconscious, but with this surge of the spirit, this

Diagram C   Horizontal & Vertical Life Progression

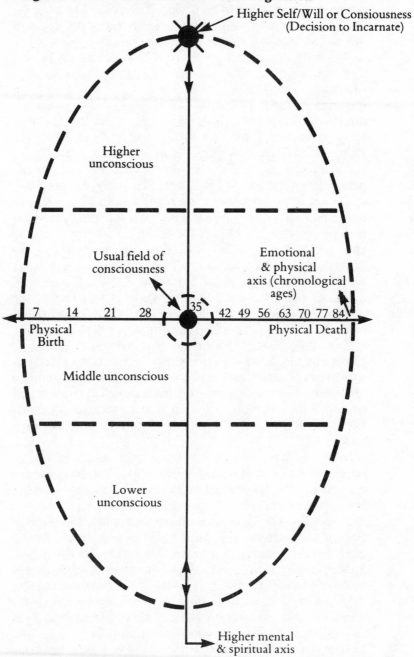

sense of purpose, I could truly see this area as a source of compost, to answer and enhance the meaning I had sought on the horizontal journey, and release the heavy sense of limitation within the little ego consciousness.

Reaching the central point from this direction, the ego consciousness was enhanced by purpose, and by a desire to continue in a state of becomingness, in order to be a growing instrument for the intentions of this Spirit, or Higher Self. It is from this sort of perspective that the little ego knows itself as the Ego with a capital 'E', and there is a glimpse of the *Self,* in the Jungian sense.

Seeing this stage of the exploration from some of the perspectives which I am here attempting to describe, opens up again the area of interface, and implies a strong movement from the purely psychological into the spiritual. To envisage a Higher Self which has consciousness and purpose for this lifetime, does not necessarily presuppose a belief in other lifetimes, but if that belief is there, then that consciousness of Higher Self, Soul, Spirit, and Purpose, also takes on a changed concept in terms of the potential breadth and depth of personal formation of, and relatedness to, a Cosmological model.

Remember that the journey of discovery is experiential. Experience leads to concept. Owning the concept alongside the experience may lead to further experience, and so on. Here I share an experience, from which I have elicited concept, and ask you to follow that concept and experience with an openness to its being an aid for your personal way.

In that which emerges then from the exercise to take an overview of your life, the suggestion is that you endeavour to see the happenings related to the horizontal axis, (physical, mental and emotional), in terms of pattern and purpose, or as holding clues to obtaining insight into that pattern and purpose. The importance of understanding lies not only with seeing or remembering the actual happenings in this reality. The events of life help us to both positive and negative awareness. We have strengths, weaknesses or survival mechanisms because of them, Seeking to know what has been made of life experience is the task now coming under consideration.

The journey of the exercise is mainly along the horizontal axis, with some time at the end to stand briefly at the other positions. It is important then to consider and visualize the diagram before beginning the exercise. The horizontal axis contains the data of actual happenings in the physical world. The vertical axis contains and opens up the potential for things related to the spiritual exploration, and the search for meaning and wholeness. As already stated the horizontal axis could be said to approximate to the physical, mental and emotional journey through life, the vertical one to the spiritual, intuitional and higher mental journey.

In this present exploration there is not intention to 'dig up' repressed material from the depths of the Lower Unconscious. The Psyche is immensely wise, and if you go gently with the flow of the experience it will only allow through that which you are able to face and deal with. Thus the memories which come into your consciousness at each stage may by no means be new, or unfamiliar or difficult. It is in asking the questions: 'Why does my psyche give me this memory now, and in this context?' and 'Why at this moment and in this context does my psyche give me this particular *series* of memories and images?' that some sense of guidance, overall purpose, and pattern will emerge. Thus the energy is not that of striving or digging but of allowing and permitting.

Deep consideration of rhythms, patterns and cycles in life, usually leads to a recognition that there are physical cycles, mental cycles, emotional cycles, and spiritual cycles. In terms of time, each one of these aspects may differ for the individual, though there may also be seen to be a certain cyclical pattern to change in one's life. A common 'mean' which is taken in considering cylical change, is that of seven years, and it seems basically that the age landmarks of 7 years, 14 years, 21 years etc. fit into peaks and troughs, realizations, and change in life.

The exercise then, looks at life in seven year periods. Preferably in a 'lying out' position, you are asked to go into your inner space, and travel to the seven year landmarks along the horizontal journey through life, starting with the point of your birth. As you pause at each age point, allow any memories or impressions, or things you have heard about that period of your life, to come into your consciousness. The endeavour is to allow one or two memories to emerge at each stage, rather than to get any detailed remembrance of the whole period. Though the stopping points are designated at 7 years, 14 years, 21 years etc., you do not need necessarily to concentrate only on these ages, but rather on anything which emerges as belonging to the period between the ages. If your personal cycles differ significantly from the seven year mean which is built into this exercise, being free to explore the *period* rather than the assumed milestone point may begin to bring insight into the specifically personal rhythms and cycles to which you are subject.

At each pause point you are receptive to that which the psyche may wish to dwell upon for the short time which is allowed. The instructions are to allow memory, feelings, thoughts, and image or symbol to emerge. Any or all of these may come into your consciousness, with varying degrees of clarity or insistence. Just accept what comes, without intellectual judgement or comment at this stage, note it down briefly, and then be prepared to move on. It is important to keep to the timing of two minutes at each pause, because this again is an overview exercise, and there will be opportunity later to work further with any aspect which has revealed itself if you wish to do so.

Remember that it may be helpful to put the instructions on tape, leaving the appropriate pauses. Make sure you will be undisturbed, have a notebook close to you, and crayons or paints and larger paper available for the end of the sequence. The instructions given below go through to age 42. If you are younger, then obviously stop at the appropriate point. (It can also be interesting to project forward to the next 'milestone age', and attempt to see what image or symbol presents itself for that future point). If you are older than 42, then continue in a similar way, until you reach your present age, or the seven year point just beyond it.

Lie down, or be in a comfortable and relaxed sitting position. Get in touch with the rhythm of your breath, let it be heart centred, but easy and relaxed. Remember that in the first part of this exploration you are going to concentrate on the physical, emotional and lower mental journey through your life up to your present age. The review of this life journey is divided into sections covering seven year cycles. You begin with the moment of your birth. . . . Sense how you feel about your birth, your choice of parents, time, place, culture into which to incarnate. . . . Be open to impressions, memories, feelings and thoughts, and see whether there is a particular image or symbol which now connects you to the time of your birth into this life. . . . You have two minutes now, to make this inquiry. . .

. . . Take a short time now to make a note of anything you have experienced, and then re-centre, ready for the next part. . .

. . . Centring back into your inner space, travel now along the line of your physical and mental journey through life, to the point where you were seven years old. Focussing around that point, but also sensing into the period from birth until age seven, be in touch with any memory, feelings or thoughts which may now arise. See whether there is an image or symbol which connects you to that period, or to the age seven milestone in your life. . . . You have two minutes for this exploration. . .

. . . Make a note now of anything which you have experienced, and wish to remember, and then be relaxed and focussed again, for the next step. . .

. . . Coming again into your inner space, relaxed and breathing from your heart centre, travel to the point in your life where you were fourteen years old. Allow any memories, feelings or thoughts to surface, which come easily, and see whether there is an image or symbol to help bring insight to that period, or to the milestone age of fourteen. . . . Spend two minutes reviewing this part of the journey. . .

. . . Allow a short time to make a note of anything you have now experienced, before centring again into your inner space. . .

. . . Move again through the rememberance of your life's journey, to the place where you were twenty one years old. Focus around this milestone age, but also around the years between fourteen and twenty one. Be in touch with any memories, feelings or thoughts which now come to you, and see whether there is an image or symbol particularly related to this age or this period of your life. . . . After two minutes, take sufficient time to make a short note of anything you wish to remember, and then relax again to prepare for the next part of the review. . .

. . . Journey now through the recollection of your life, to the point where you were twenty eight years old. Let the energy of your heart centre around this age, but also give attention to the

years from twenty one to twenty eight, and allow memories, feelings or thoughts to come into your consciousness. Seek an image or symbol which helps to link you to this age or life period, and after two minutes, take time to make a brief note...

...Relaxed and centred again, travel now to the point in your life where you were thirty five years old. Recall this age, but also the period between twenty eight and thirty five years. Be with the memories, feelings and thoughts of that period, and see whether there is an appropriate image or symbol relating to this time. After two minutes, go again to your notepad, to make brief notes of anything you now want to retain...

... Centre within once more, and travel along the line of your physical and mental journey through life until you reach the point where you were forty two years old. Focus into this milestone age, but also review the period between thirty five and forty two years. Be with any memories, feelings or thoughts which now arise. Seek an image or symbol to help you to relate to that phase or your life. After two minutes give yourself time to make any brief notes you require...

(If the instructions have now covered the full period of your life, proceed to the following stage of the review. Otherwise continue your life recall in seven year stages until you are ready to add this stage as a completion to the exercise.)

For the final time find the position in which you are centred and relaxed, and breathe with the energy of your heart. The journey which you have just made through your life remembrances, may be seen as the horizontal axis of a cross. Imagine now, that you stand in contact with the vertical axis of the cross, and get a sense of your spiritual, intuitive, and higher mental journey through your life. Experience this axis in your own way, travelling freely along it. Sense if you can, any connection it gives between your Higher Self or Soul, and the present actuality of your incarnation. Feel into the energy of each end of this axis, and also that of the centre. As you travel to these points, see whether there is additional information in symbol, image, or thought, which can help in giving meaning to the horizontal axis of your life journey. Spend five minutes in this exploration, and then return to a sense of your body lying or sitting in whichever physical place you have chosen to be. Feel your breath in your heart centre, open your eyes, and make full contact with your physical environment. Stretch, move your body, stand up, and feel the contact of your feet with the ground. Make any notes you need to make, but then take a break for tea, or coffee, or a meal before reflecting further on any information you have received from the whole of this overview.

Sharing the memories, images and symbols, and anything you have written or drawn in relationship to this stage of the exploration, with a friend or partner will help to bring insights and recognitions. Do not work too hard to understand intellectually, especially with the symbols. Be prepared to 'stay alongside' what has emerged, and to let an evolution of understanding happen over a period. Symbols which the psyche gives during this sort of exploration have a healing value and life of their own. Some of them may immediately enhance your vision of yourself, others may seem more remote. All of them are a part of you, and your inner life and potential. Their accepted emergence is significant in itself. Decoding, analysis and interpretation are secondary at this stage. (There is more comment on the language of symbols on page 141).

The next stage of the journey towards guidance, is to use the power of the inner landscape and its symbolism to help to heal and transform, and to release psychic energy.

For this inner experience the help of a talisman is again required (See page 41) there may be a new talisman for this new part of the journey, or you may call upon a familiar one, or perhaps both will be present.

The objective now is to combine some of the information which has been gathered from the explorations described in this chapter. Reference is being made then to the exploration of the four elements in the inner landscape, and to the building and recognition of that landscape. Some of the areas by their very description imply a certain heaviness or negativity, e.g. The Pit; the Rocky Path etc. While others such as the Tree of Life; the Waters of Peace etc. have more positive implications. To a large degree the negative or positive experience of the symbols and areas will be subjective, though there is an evaluatory weight given to them by the very descriptions which are used. A choice of a 'negative' and a 'positive' area of the inner landscape is to be made.

To embark on this exercise then go back to your

drawings or descriptions, your 'map' of the inner landscape, and make a choice of two areas, one which is more
negative for you, and one which is more positive. Look at
them and note the possible routes from one area to the
other. In the magic carpet journey over the inner landscape
you noted positions, but did not actually enter specifically
into the atmosphere of any of the things encountered. In
this part of the journey you will be asked to journey to the
areas of your choice. If this sort of work is new to you, it is
perhaps wise not to immediately select an area which you
suspect may be of major confrontation to you. Once you
sense the healing aspect of the exercise you can repeat it
using other combinations, but always working to your
own pace. In selecting and allowing you own pace there is
an important ingredient which is very relevant to the
opening of inner guidance and to preparing the pathway to
discarnate guidance. This is the ingredient of self respect
linked to self responsibility. There is often a temptation to
want to move too quickly, to confront that which is not
necessarily ready to be confronted. I have already said that
the psyche is very wise, and I repeat this. If you try to go
too fast you will meet with resistance which may prove
very difficult to overcome. If you push too hard against
your initial and natural defences without due feeling and
reverence for the wisdom of the psyche in producing these
defences then you may be confronted too quickly with
some of the inner depths of your consciousness. When you
meet resistance honour it, explore the reasons for it and
gently journey beyond it only when you feel ready to do
so. There is a core running through many of us which
seems to say that the medicine must be nasty in order to be
effective; the pathway must be hard and confronting in
order to be worthwhile; initiation is a difficult and danger-
ous experience. I believe that to some extent it is these
attitudes which need to be questioned and confronted so
that the way forward to the enlargement of spiritual
horizons and experience can be as joyful as the goal, and
the journey may be one of love and healing rather than of
flagellation, pain and suffering.

Choose then the areas of your inner landscape for use in
this exercise with full consciousness and self compassion.
When you have journeyed to the area you will be asked to

experience the atmosphere of it for a short time, and then to try to link with any of the life memories you evoked during your journey along the horizontal axis of your life. For instance, for me the desert is an arid and negative area linked with periods in my life when I get out of touch with my feelings, and become the victim of my own dry intellectual overdrive. To go to the inner desert almost always evokes specific memories of such times, but through increasing knowledge of my inner landscape I know that there are oases in the desert, and also that sometimes I need the energy of balance which the desert can give if I am in danger of imbalance in the opposite direction. Sinking into the bog of emotional depression, for example, which is also one of my tendencies.

The exercise for which this discussion is a lead-in is designed to bring facility in using the inner dimension to give positive tools and techniques of balance to help in managing the requirements of outer life.

When you are ready to embark on this part of the journey make sure, as before that you will be undisturbed. Have a notebook, and some crayons and large paper to hand to record your experience. Before you begin look at the pictures you drew of your inner landscape. (See Page 45). Consider which 'positive' area and which 'negative' area you are willing to contact more closely during the course of this journey. As you look at your drawing get a sense of the route between the two, the way to go to journey particularly from the negative area of your choice to the positive one.

I now give the instructions for this exercise in such a form that you can record them onto tape if you wish, or perhaps ask a friend or partner to read them to you as you relax into your inner space.

. . . Sit or lie comfortably. Make sure that you will be warm enough for the duration of the exercise, which is about 30 minutes. Let your body be relaxed but poised and symmetrical . . . contact the rhythm of your breath and feel that rhythm in your heart centre . . . let your heart centre gently unfold and open to the rhythm of each in-breath and each out-breath. . . . As your heart centre opens, be again in your inner space, perhaps poised over your inner landscape, or in a quiet meadow. . . . Make sure that you have a talisman with you, perhaps a familiar

one, or maybe a special one for this particular journey . . . and when you are ready go to the positive area which you chose when you looked at your inner landscape drawing before the beginning of this exercise . . . be in this place, as fully as possible in your inner space . . . know its colours and objects . . . feel its textures . . . hear its sounds . . . smell its fragrances . . . and taste its tastes. . . . As you establish yourself here, remember the journey which you made through the stages of your life, and see if any particular memories linked to that journey are also specifically linked to this pleasant place in your inner landscape . . . be with those memories here, and see whether any particular image or symbol is evoked for you. . . . Take three minutes to be with these memories, images or symbols in this place. . .

. . . Now, making sure that your talisman is with you, journey from this place to the more negative place in your landscape which you feel able to explore . . . journey there, and go into its atmosphere, and as you do so see whether this place relates to any particular memory or group of memories from your life . . . see whether there are images or symbols linked to this place for you. . . . Take two minutes for this part of the exploration, and as you stay in this place feel the strength of the talisman with you. . .

. . . It is the energy of the talisman which can now help you to prepare to leave this area of your landscape, and to return to the positive place where you began, but first, look around this area again, and see whether it could be given any attention . . . maybe a bog needs draining . . . a dark place needs light . . . an arid place needs an oasis . . . a colourless place needs colour . . . note these possibilities before you leave, and then journey with your talisman to the positive place in your landscape where you have been before . . . when you get to the positive area, look again at the memory or incident or group of memories which the negative place evoked, and see whether they have the same power over you in this positive area . . . concentrate now particularly on the symbols and images which are linked to the positive and negative memories and places, and prepare to take these symbols to another positive place in your landscape . . . this time to a particular place of wisdom or peace, perhaps to your sanctuary . . . any positive place which is different from the one where you now are, and where you sense you may get access to wisdom or insight or healing . . . journey now . . . with your talisman and images, memories and symbols to this other place of your choice. . .

. . . In the place where you now are, invoke wisdom, or healing, or insight, and ask for a new symbol or message, or 'inner knowing' which can help you, in future, to detach from negative patterns in your life, and contact your inner resources of strength and empowerment. . . . It may be that a figure will be drawn to you as you invoke healing, insight, and wisdom, to give you a message or a symbol or just a sense of inner reassurance . . . stay in this place for three minutes, being receptive to positive energies of change. . .

. . . When you return, it can help to spend a few moments lying in the foetal position, just to anchor your experiences, and to allow time for coming back to the normal dimension of everyday life. . . . Make some sort of record of your journey, memories, symbols, and the connections you made.

In this exploration the suggestion has been introduced that there may have been an inner figure, in your inner world, connected with wisdom or healing. It is now time to write further of my personal experiences and to consider more directly issues of inner and discarnate guidance, and their definition and differentiation.

CHAPTER 3

Mainly About Inner Guidance

The full story of my own experiences is told in *'Gildas Communicates'*; *'Seven Inner Journeys'*; and *'The Healing Spectrum'*; (all published by C. W. Daniel Ltd.), but it is perhaps useful here to summarise those experiences, and give definition to the name and personality of 'Gildas', and his relationship to me.

'Gildas' is the name of the presence who is always near me, whom I identify as my discarnate guide. That is to say that I experience him as a separate personality, being, or entity, communicating from another plane of existence, and not from or part of a solely inner part of myself. I understand him (also by his own definition) to have been incarnate many times on the earth plane, but to be now in a discarnate state.

I am aware that this presence was with me from my earliest childhood. I did not know him then as 'Gildas', or as a 'guide'. Since he either appears wearing a white monkish robe, or in his glowing 'energy' body, and since adults speak sometimes to children of 'guardian angels', if I thought about him, or questioned his presence at all, it was to assume he was an angel.

As well as awareness of this companion I saw the fairies and elementals in the garden. I saw the house fairies, and the fairies which come when there is laughter, dancing or live music. I saw the changing colours, and energy fields or auras around people and material objects.

It only dawned on me very gradually that the expanded world of which I was conscious was not only in some way 'different', but that it was questionable and unacceptable. The older I grew the more adults frowned upon my 'strange' perceptions, and comments. I became bewildered and withdrawn, and was considered to be a 'difficult' child.

My task in this life is concerned with inner perception, and perhaps partly to signal this I was born with little sight in my right eye. As I cut off from my inner vision in order to find the way to work with the standards and beliefs expected of me, so my left eye became more and more short sighted, until eye specialists were ready to declare me partially sighted with a probability of early blindness. My ambition to study languages to an advanced standard was considered impossible. I was advised to leave my books and work outdoors with plants. Eventually a compromise was reached and I went to train as an Infants' teacher.

Bewilderment was still a keynote for me as I arrived for training, but quite unconsciously in making my choice of course, I had been accepted at the only teachers' college (over 30 years ago) which had facilities for student counselling. It soon became apparent that I was a candidate for such counselling, and I met Mary Swainson, not only a pioneer in Student Counselling, and a Jungian Therapist, but with esoteric insight and training. (Author of 'The Spirit of Counsel', Pub. C. W. Daniel.)

With Mary's quiet acceptance, concern and encouragement my inner world began gradually to unfold. Instead of confirming my worst fears, that I must be mad or deluded, she spoke to me of my giftedness, and of the need to develop these faculties. As I gained in confidence, so my eyesight stabilised, and ceased to give cause for anxiety.

So Gildas emerged fully into my consciousness, and I now know him not as an angel*, but as a discarnate guide and companion. I see him usually in his energy body full of pink, violet, white and gold colours of light, though in the early days of his reappearance I saw him more often as a monk in a white robe.

Almost all that he has said about himself is that during his final incarnation he was a Benedictine Monk in 14th century France, and that now he is part of a group from the 'other side', who are seeking to help individuals in incarnation on earth, and also the planet of earth itself. He, and presumably the group of which he speaks are concerned with teaching, guidance and healing, they bring an input from their perspective which carries a message of urgency but also of hope.

I am often asked what it is like to have this constant

---

* *angel - see Glossary.*

guide and companion. I feel Gildas' presence always with me, and it takes only a few moments to 'shift' consciousness and be in communication with him. I experience his voice rather than hearing it, and receive his words like a sort of dictation. For at least twenty five years I wrote these words down, and usually someone else read out what had been written. This was partly because there is a very shy and reticent side to my nature, and the thought of speaking to groups, either large or small, in spite of my teaching experience was not easy. Eventually I developed severe writers' cramp, and realised I should have to use a tape recorder if Gildas' teaching was to continue. The transition was easier than I had thought, and now almost all messages are spoken directly, and recorded if necessary. It is obvious that Gildas feels much less restricted with this method, and can more easily explain some of the complexities of the view from his perspective.

It is my experience that the true guides have a wonderful sense of humour. When in contact with us they have access again to the earth environment, without its limitations and pains and anguish. Gildas seems to delight in some of the modern inventions, and says that he enjoys our ability to reproduce colours and textures. He brings a high level of vitality with him, and I feel energized rather than drained by his presence, and from being his channel for communication.

In the early days it was lonely. This may seem a strange statement following my description of the vital and constant presence of Gildas. Thirty years ago though, it was not easy to speak of these things. At age nineteen I was young to be entering into 'mediumship'. I did not know anyone else who had similar experiences, and no one except Mary, then my therapist, who could accept, value and understand them.

I actually use Gildas for my own guidance and decisions far less than is often supposed. I have always felt a need to maintain my independence, separateness and identity, and he has encouraged this. I have sometimes taken a rather stubborn independence to extremes, and learned the long and hard way, rather than asking for or following advice. I am more tractable now, but do not regret my independence, and feel that it has helped me to form a relationship with Gildas which is full of what he calls 'creative tension', and is neither 'empty' nor subservient on my part.

Being independent in my nature and therefore in my way of working with Gildas has meant that as well as having my discarnate guide I have had to learn more of my own inner nature, and of my inner resources for guidance, and decision making. There is no doubt that Gildas has had a strong influence on my philosophy of life or my personal 'cosmology', but as I have considered the best way in which to help others to find clear guidance, so I come more and more to feel that my personal journey has had many parts of it in reverse to that which is the gentler developmental direction.

My discarnate guidance, this relationship with Gildas, was 'given' without asking for it at the level of the personality incarnate in this lifetime. To come to a practical and as near as possible 'normal' way of living I have had to 'desensitize' myself. In order to feel creative and fulfilled in my true self, and especially as a woman, I have had to learn to avoid being too much the 'channel', totally reliant on 'what Gildas says', existing only as a medium for him.

Yet because I find Gildas' philosophical teachings exciting and important, I am also willingly the channel for his desire to reach out and help those who are on a conscious path of exploration whilst in incarnation. I am sufficiently in tune with his purpose, for it to be relevant to my own view of *my* purpose. This relevance is essential in enabling me to move towards a co-partnership relationship with Gildas, and to develop and use my personal skills in the work too.

In the journey to guidance, this point at which there is sufficient self-containment to consider purpose, and to take responsibility for that purpose is vital. It is not enough to desire or know or to have a discarnate guide. We are moving from the Piscean Age to the Aquarian Age in astrological terms, and relationship to discarnate guidance is changing and maturing.

It is this point which makes all the difference between mere channelling of discarnates, (the Piscean model of mediumship), and the hope in the Aquarian model for a real cooperation between the levels and planes of experience. The self knowledge, the self containment and strength come not from the discarnate guides, but from the inner guidance system. The points of reference and wisdom and detachment are found (mainly) in the field covered by Transpersonal Psychology, or just into the interface area which I have already attempted to define.

Gildas took an active part in helping me to find my own inner strength, but he could not give it to me directly. The danger of the experience coming in the pattern in which it came to me, is the over reliance on the discarnate guide, the giving away of power, the loss of discrimination about the material given, and the way in which guidance should be interpreted and used. I see it as part of the guidance system in operation in my life that I was led to Mary Swainson, by a series of 'coincidences' and synchronous happenings. This meant that my psychological needs were diagnosed and supported. Knowing and 'clearing' myself became as important as the development of the contact with Gildas, but also an integral part of it.

Thus, exploration of the inner guidance system becomes a desirable preliminary to contact with discarnate guidance. The sense of companionship and wider purpose and perspective which can come from discarnate contact arises most safely and naturally from the strongest, wisest or highest point of inner guidance, self knowledge, and self respect.

There is a paradox which becomes apparent here. Often those who are desparate for guidance from a discarnate source *are* so desperate because the sense of self and inner trust is either undeveloped or has broken down. In many ways this is the least desirable time to be receiving guidance, since too much authority is given over to the guidance source, and self responsibility for action is not sufficiently present. When one is strong in one's self, the desire for discarnate communication or guidance becomes less intense, but it is at or from this point that the discarnate contact is likely to break through.

Gildas has often said to those seeking to know their guides:

'Your guide may not approach you until you are stronger in yourself. From where you now stand you would give all responsibility to your guide, and cease to take in your life lessons at a conscious level, or to develop your own inner strength. When you come to a place of conscious choice then your own guide can add perspective, guidance and support.'

When giving guidance to others Gildas works from a position of teaching rather than from clairvoyance or direction. He endeavours to give input which is seen from his perspective and not from ours' in order that the available information relating to decision making can be expanded and deepened. He will often say,

'Given this perspective the way in which you could move becomes clearer, but I cannot make the decisions for you, I can only give wider reference points to your essential choice.'

He sees possibilities and potentials, but cannot of himself set those possibilities and potentials in motion, nor guarantee that all things will come together in such a way that definitive, foreseeable things will happen. In this way, because there is freedom of will it seems that only a proportion of the future can really be seen or known, there are so many permutations of choice, particularly in relationships.

This sort of guidance needs to be met from a point of inner strength. Often by an energy which it seems to carry it will enable that strength. Often through the glimpse of the wider perspective there comes an inner relaxation. The wider version gives help in coming to more meaningful decisions. The learning situations of life are seen more clearly and with greater acceptance.

There is a lot of confusion, and anxiety about definitions of inner and discarnate guidance, and also about levels of guidance. The latter phrase, 'levels of guidance', mainly applies in my model to discarnate guidance, and there will be discussion about this in the next chapter. Definition as to whether the guidance being contacted is inner or discarnate comes largely from experience, but can be structured in the design of the preparatory exercise or meditation and by intent and invocation.

Clear guidance, either inner or discarnate is another matter. There is always the danger of adulteration by personal belief, hang up or emotion. The way to self awareness and discrimination comes through opening to inner adventure and discovery. Certainty is built up through experience, and step by step greater transparency comes.

It is necessary to define the terms 'colouring' and 'transparency'. The former relates to the ways in which that which is heard or received as guidance can all too often have tones of parents, or teachers, or other authority and power. There may even be echoes of the inner saboteur, which often resides within. Transparency relates to the state where there is relative detachment from the common messages within or around, so that certainty in guidance can really give that lift to another level of clarity in decision making, or in helping relationship to others and to life itself.

Contacting inner figures which personify archetypal energy, or which are sub-personalities within the psyche are ways both of discovering and clearing vulnerability towards colouring and also of identifying and contacting aspects of the inner guidance 'system'.

In my view there is a system of inner guidance, inter-relating with areas of potential and vulnerability from which a comprehensive picture of insight may be built up. There are, naturally 'levels' within this system, but all have a specific validity in forming the picture, or a place in the 'team'. In discarnate guidance 'levels' have another meaning and significance, and protection and direction are very necessary factors. These will be discussed later in the text.

Before contacting inner archetypal and sub-personality figures with the specific intention of seeking guidance, it is well to come to a consciousness of the specific areas for which you are seeking guidance. In order to build up a picture of the inner system, a specific question which can be taken to its various layers or levels is useful.

The exercise of going through the seven year life cycles may have given clarity about where guidance is required. It may be in relationship to patterns which tend to be negatively repetitive, in relationship to healing, or to defining affirmation or action.

Emphasis in inner world exploration is heavily on 'right brain', and the intuition. Creative guidance often comes from intuitive levels, and right brain activation. In my view though, it is wise to retain a balance, and not to put aside levels of thinking, and mental reviewing too easily. In the Western world there has been a tendency to over evaluate thinking as a function, but there is a need not to go to another polarity in the mistaken assumption that this will form balance. Polarisation is reaction, rather than balance. True guidance leads from polarity to synthesis.

The next exercise which I give then is an exercise in formulating questions, but also in bringing a balance of thought and mentally 'working it out', with creative or intuitive insight.

Finding the right question to ask can be an exercise in guidance itself. The present search asks that you keep in mind any insights which have been gained so far, if you are following the process outlined in this book. It begins with three questions for consideration:

'Where am I now?'

'What are my guidance needs?'

'What question(s) should I be asking now?

When I say 'for consideration', I mean exactly that. Take some time and a piece of paper, and consider in a *thinking* way what your answers are to these three questions.

'Where am I now?' will help you to assess where you feel yourself to be, right now, on life's journey; how you feel yourself to be in relationship to that journey. Write down anything that comes, but try to be consciouus also of a rational thought and relating process in coming to your answers or conclusions.

'What are my guidance needs?' will help you to see the areas in which guidance is required. Are you seeking action, healing, changed attitudes, affirmations to help you in every day living? Again stay, at this stage with a thinking process, but write down whatever comes, even if it seems flippant or irrelevant.

'What question(s) should I be asking now?' may lead you, through looking at the process in relationship to the two

previous questions to be able to formulate a specific question. As you attempt to formulate questions you may become aware that you know the answers already, and therefore need to move towards a new question. In putting the 's' of the word question in brackets, I am strongly suggesting that you aim towards one question, with perhaps a subsidiary. This is an exercise in focus, discipline and precision. It is better at the end of this part to remain with the question 'What question should I be asking now?' than to have a whole list of questions.

Ideally at this stage comes a sharing of this thinking and reflective process with a friend or partner, who will react to the conclusions you have reached with interest, but perhaps also with constructive questioning which will lead you further.

The next stage in formulating the question which will be present in your exploration of the inner guidance system is to allow the intuitional or right brain aspect to make its comment or accretion in the process. For this you again need quietness, some crayons, and three sheets of paper. As timing is involved either put the instructions on tape, leaving the appropriate time gap as required between stages, or ask someone to cooperate in giving the instructions and being the timekeeper.

The objective so far has been to work through a thinking and reasoning level with these three questions. Material from previous exercises helps orientation. Now there is the opportunity to allow the right brain or intuitive levels to give comment. The method is through use of intuitive drawing and calling on the energy of the heart centre or chakra. The instructions help you to experience the particular orientation of the heart chakra. Surrounded by that energy you begin to sense images, symbols, energy patterns or colours which come into your consciousness. You then attempt to draw or in some way express on your paper, preferably without words, the responses you receive from this level to the questions. As this is intuitive drawing three minutes only is allowed for the response to each question. If you are interested in drawing you may want to perfect it later but the aim is to stay with what comes first, and to anchor an impression of that. There is an orientation time, then two minutes to allow the inner process to begin, and then three minutes with the paper and crayons. Here are the instructions as I give them in workshops:

Find a place in which you know you can be comfortable and relaxed. Have three sheets of paper at hand (one for each question), and some crayons. . . . Lie down if you wish to and begin by relaxing your body. . . . Make it balanced and symmetrical. . . . Be in touch with the rhythm of your breath, and feel that breath in the centre of your body, at a level with your physical heart, but in the centre. . . this is the area of the heart chakra or centre. . . . Breathe rhythmically in and out through your heart centre, and let your awareness focus around the question 'Where am I now?' *. . . let go the mental process relating to this question, and ask for symbols, energy forms or colour. . . be open to the flow, and as soon as you feel ready, keeping the rhythm of breath in your heart centre, and a meditative space around you, move to your paper and crayons, and let the work on the paper be part of the process in your heart centre. . . you have three minutes now for drawing. . . .* (Leave space on your tape).

Leave your drawing now, and put your second piece of paper to hand. . . be in touch again with the rhythm of your breath, and through it with the energy of your heart. . . let your breath go in and out through your heart centre. . . let the consciousness of your heart focus around the question 'What are my guidance needs?' *. . .let go of the previous process relating to this question and ask for symbols, energy forms or colour. . . open yourself to another way of perceiving the response to the question, and when you feel ready, staying in the heart energy and the meditative space around you, take your paper and crayons, and continue the work on the paper, in colour. . . you have three minutes now for the drawing. . .* (Leave space on your tape).

Once more leave your drawing and put your third piece of paper to hand . . . let your body relax, and breathe in and out through your heart centre, activating the energy of the heart. . . let the awareness of your heart be centred on the question 'What question, or questions should I be asking now?' *. . .open yourself for the input of symbols, or colour or energy patterns, and when you are ready take your paper and continue the open creative process in colour and drawing, keeping the heart emphasis, and the meditational space around you. . . there are three minutes for your drawing. . .* (leave space on your tape).

67

When you have finished the drawings, go back to any notes you made about the thinking and reasoning stages and put these alongside the drawings. Again it helps if you have someone with whom you can discuss the process, but if not spend some time allowing yourself to absorb these things before going on to the next parts of the journey.

As what has been gathered together with the help of these questions consolidates there may now emerge a sense or overview as to what guidance could mean, and what you expect or require from it. You may have a formulated question to take forward to the next stage.

This next stage is further exploration of the inner guidance system. 'Further', because reviewing the process so far it can be seen that there is potential guidance, resolution, or healing even from the symbolism of the inner landscape, and a wise person or inner figure may already have emerged briefly.

Levels of relaxing, and letting that which 'comes' emerge into consciousness in the form of memory or image, as in the stage of life exercise, is also a means of contacting the inner guidance system.

In a later chapter there is comment on dreams, so if you do not already do so it could be interesting to start recording your dreams from this point onwards, with a view to seeing how they too amplify and substantiate inner guidance.

The present concern though is that of meeting various inner figures. In the course of guided journeys these figures may have a spectrum of comments to make. Asking of them symbolic gifts may help insight, initiative, acceptance or decision making.

A brief definition of 'archetypes' from the Oxford Dictionary, has already been given: 'Primordial images inherited by all'. It is now necessary to amplify this, in order to understand how personified archetypes in the inner worlds form part of the guidance system, and to be subsequently able to clarify definition of the transpersonal psychological term 'sub-personalities'.

Archetypal energies are all around us all the time, forming an important part of understanding the world and relationship to it. Words like 'peace' and 'justice' need little definition, but in themselves imply archetypes. There may be an awareness that these two words mean slightly different things to different races or cultures, yet most civilizations develop some specific systems or purposes which are strongly motivated by the urge to peace or the urge to justice. These and other archetypal concerns, energies or drives, in constant subtle or overt presence affect us both consciously and unconsciously.

When an archetypal drive is held in consciousness it can provide purpose, satisfaction, motivation, and emotive energy. The positive archetypes always have their negative counterparts. It is possible to come up with a very long and comprehensive list of archetypal forces or images. Tarot cards, for instance, in the major arcana carry twenty two archetypal images or figures including Justice, but not Peace, Death but not Birth. In Tarot, The World, and The Devil are seen as archetypes.

On the other hand there can be a very reduced list of archetypes, essentially positive, from which all the others evolve, or to which they are related. I would suggest: God; Peace; The World; Power; Justice; Healing; Beauty; Wisdom; The Angelic and Devic Kingdoms, and Love.

As stated, each positive has a negative, or there is a negative as well as a positive interpretation possible for those which have no apparent opposite. Often the archetypal drives are not held sufficiently in consciousness, but in the words of C. G. Jung:

'They are images sprung from the life, the joys and sorrows, of our ancestors; to live they seek to return, not in experience only, but in deed. Because of their opposition to the conscious mind they cannot be translated straight into our world; hence a way must be found that can mediate between conscious and unconscious reality.'

The archetypes affect us collectively, racially and individually. They are projected outwardly onto others, especially public figures, politicians, leaders, gurus. These public figures often carry a great weight of projection, and partly because of this unless they are exceptionally dedicated and clear sighted, the archetypes can often invade, inflate or exhaust those who are in responsible or leadership positions. The more that every individual can own responsibility, strength and power, and cease to hand these things over to the various 'theys' of authority, the more likely we are to find clear sighted leaders who reflect the highest energies of those whom they seek to lead and to serve. If leaders are either exalted as heroes/heroines, or disliked/hated out of all proportion then they have to be special indeed to act disinterestedly for the common good.

It is also possible for leaders or others to work consciously with the archetypal forces, images or energies so that they are empowered and energised by them, using them to enhance and balance personal vision of that which is for the common good. When there is a conscious harnessing of archetypal power, a 'flowing with it', then there is a magical dimension to life, and its positive possibilities become endless, yet reachable.

Let me substantiate what I am saying by speaking more personally. In the nature of my work I am subject to the projection from others of the archetypes of Power, the Priestess, or the Guru. It would therefore be possible to be invaded by these archetypes, to believe that I *am* them because other people sometimes see me in this way. Being alive to this possibility keeps me aware of when the projection is happening. It is not always comfortable, but to the degree to which I can accept or analyse the need to use the archetypal energy to help to heal, to teach, or to give insight, I keep the energy in consciousness. In doing this I then work with the archetypes without identifying with them, and open up the possibility to hand back the projection, at the right moment, so that people may find in themselves that which they have seen temporarily mirrored in me.

That which applies to the collective or the general also applies within the inner organization of the psyche. The macrocosm is reflected in the microcosm, and vice versa. Much of what Jung calls the the way that 'must be found that can mediate between conscious and unconscious reality' begins for the collective, within the individual psyche. When it is found and honoured in the individual psyche then each being grows towards potential and empowerment.

Acknowledgement of, and dialogue with the archetypes, or archetypal images can thus form an interesting and useful part of the inner guidance system. I have mentioned some archetypes, and also the Major Arcana of the Tarot cards. The next exercise which I shall give is concerned with the choice of an archetype to meet. Here is the list of archetypes from the Tarot cards, plus some other suggestions for an expanded list. Consider them and see whether there is an appropriate archetype which it might be valuable for you to meet at this time.

The Fool; The Magician; The Priestess; The Empress; The Emperor; the Priest; The Lovers; The Chariot; Strength; The Hermit; The Wheel of Fortune; Justice; The Hanged Man; Death; Temperance; The Devil; The Tower, The Star; The Moon; The Sun; Judgement; The World. (These are the twenty two archetypal images of the Major Arcana in Tarot. Terminology will differ slightly from pack to pack, and teacher to teacher.)

Some additions I have suggested already, or rather some basic archetypes from which the others spring, but I would suggest in a fuller list that there are also: The Hero; The Victim; The Eternal Child; The Witch; The Pilgrim; The Guru; The Pupil; The Teacher; The Father; The Mother; Compassion; Mercy; Suffering; The Explorer.

There are many others, but this list will probably suffice to give some idea of the range. Do not worry if you are unacquainted with this sort of symbolism. Feel into what the archetypes mean for you. Your choice does not have to be from the lists given. Your own feeling and intuitive response is what is important, and is the point from which the journey towards constructive guidance begins.

Consider these lists of archetypes alongside any question which has evolved or become specific for you at this point. Consider which one you feel may have some meaning or message for you in relationship to your life pattern at this time, or in relationship to your question. Spend some time 'being alongside' this before embarking on the next stage in the exploration.

This next stage is a guided inner journey to meet with the archetypal image or personification of your choice. It is extremely important that you choose, before making this journey the specific archetype you wish to meet. Do not go into this journey with the sense of inviting the one which wants to speak to you to come. In inner, and discarnate guidance it is very important to know that you are in charge of the process, and can limit it or stop it and return at any point where you feel you have gone far enough for the time being.

The archetypal forces are powerful, you have only to read through the lists given to see this. Therefore a limitation is built into this exercise by making a prior choice. If you want to repeat the journey, with an invitation to another archetype, to get another view on your question etc. that is perfectly in order, but the rule here is one at a time, with prior, rational choice as to which it is to be.

Making this prior choice will not limit the form which the archetype will take, or the symbolic information which the psyche may give you, but it will ensure that you meet only the archetype you feel ready to meet, and only one at a time.

This is, in part, the meaning of the words 'intent', and 'invocation', already mentioned. They are linked to choice and responsibility. They help you to make as much of the journey as you want to make, and are prepared for at any one time. To a great extent what you invoke, you will meet; your journey will form itself around your intent. There is both challenge and safety in this knowledge. Rightly used it can ensure that you journey from a point of choice and this is an important and basic offering from your outer self to your inner worlds, and therefore to finding help and wisdom within.

There is usually a central figure in the inner guidance system of each individual, representing purely the Inner Wise Being. This being too is an archetype, and may be related to the archetype of Wisdom or of Guidance, though may seem to some extent closer to a sub personality (see page 78). In this journey about to be described you will go first to the dwelling place of the Inner Wise Being, and see whether this being wishes to accompany you to the archetype, or whether there is any useful advice for the enterprise. The being may also have some useful comment to make on any question you are taking with you.

Another useful companion or source of strength and inspiration for the journey may be the talisman. Remember that though you have perhaps obtained your talisman before, and this may remain constant for you in your inner journeys and meditations, there is sometimes an additional talisman, for a specific journey. It is always wise to check again, or invoke this sort of help and provision at an early stage in the excursion.

When you feel settled with your question, (it may still remain as 'what question should I be asking now?'), and you have made your choice as to the archetype you wish to meet, prepare for the journey to meet the Inner Wise being and the archetype.

During the course of this exercise you will also be given an instruction about meeting with your power animal. The concept of this animal is related to early cultures, and is particularly emphasised in the North American Indian and Shamanic traditions. It can be an important ally to establish in the inner guidance system, because through contact with the power animal energy is released from the lower chakras*, in particular the Root and the Sacral chakras. Harnessing this energy in the form of a meeting with a power animal is a very safe way to do it, and it means that all your instinctual awareness goes with you on the journey. The power animal can be absolutely any animal in existence, and is sometimes a mythological animal. In the natural environment the animal which appears as your power animal may well be very wild and fierce. In the world of your inner landscape it is your guardian, protector and friend. It may or may not have the power of speech, but you will probably feel very basically in communication with it. Try not to think too much about this potential animal before doing the exercise, because it needs to be the first one that comes to you in the particular inner world situation into which the instructions lead you. The animal you meet may surprise you, but most people feel very happy with this meeting, and often very empowered by it. Knowing and accepting the power animal can bring about many subtle life changes. Symbolism relating to different animals and animal groups will be commented on later.

Have a notebook, paper and crayons available for recording. It is often helpful to lie out for this sort of journey. If you are going to do so make sure that you will be warm enough, by having a rug to wrap up in, as there is a tendency to lose body heat when relaxed, and focussed

* *See Page 100 and glossary.*

on the inner worlds. Once again I will give the instructions for the exercise in such a way that you can pre-record them onto a tape, or get a friend to read them out for you. The journey will take about 30 minutes.

. . . *Get in touch with the rhythm of your breath. . . . Feel your breath in your heart centre, and breathe in and out through that centre, which is in the middle of your body on a level with the physical heart. . . . As you relax remember your intent in making this exploration, and the specific archetype you wish to meet . . . invoke the angelic qualities of light and love and healing to be present with you for this journey, and gradually find yourself in your inner space in a meadow. . . . Take the opportunity of being in the meadow to use your inner senses . . . see the objects and the colours . . . hear the sounds . . . feel the textures . . . smell the fragrances . . . and taste the tastes. . .*

. . . *Look down at yourself and see how you are dressed for the exploration and ask for any appropriate talisman, either already known or specific to the journey to be with you. . . . Know that you are going first to the dwelling place of the inner wise being, look around the meadow and find the roadway or path which you will know is the one to lead you to this dwelling place. . . . In the next three minutes of silence, journey along that way until you come to the place where your inner wise being lives. . . .* (Leave a space of three minutes here on your tape).

. . . *When you have arrived at the home of the wise being, invoke that being's presence . . . perhaps you will be invited into the house . . . perhaps you will walk a little way together to where there is a view over the landscape . . . perhaps you will sit down together near water. . . . See who your wise being is . . . whether they are masculine or feminine, and how they are dressed. . . . Tell your wise being of your intention to visit the archetype of your choice, and of the question that you are taking to this meeting with you. . . . If you feel at ease with your wise being and it seems appropriate to do so, ask whether he/she will accompany you to the meeting place with the archetype. . . . In any case ask whether the wise being has any instructions for you about the way, anything you should take, and any comment himself/herself on your question. . . .* (There are four minutes in which to have this interchange, if you are making a tape leave four minutes space here).

. . .*Whether your wise being is to accompany you on the next stage or not, you now need to ask to meet with your power* animal. . . . *Remember that this animal is one which in normal circumstances may be very wild untamed or ferocious, but in your inner space it represents an instinctual power, and is your guardian and protector with whom you are able to communicate. . .*

. . . *Your power animal will probably come to you from a cave, perhaps a cave near water. . . . Ask your inner wise being to take you now to the place where you can meet with your power animal. . . . You do not need to go into the power animal's cave . . . together with your wise being you can call your power animal to you, but you may need to go together to the place where you can see the cave from which the animal will come. . . . Take the next three minutes to invite your power animal to come to you, in order to accompany you on the rest of this journey to the archetype. . . .* (Leave a three minute space on your tape here. . .).

. . . *When you have greeted your power animal you will be ready to continue to the meeting place with the archetype. . . . Your power animal will now accompany you, and maybe your wise being. . . . You still have your talisman, and any advice or gift your wise being may have given you for the journey. . . . Ahead of you the path leads on up a mountain, and you are going to a plateau which is near the top of the mountain, but not right at the top of it. . . . With your companions, climb the path to the plateau now, noticing the landscape and the route you are taking as you go. . .* (Leave two minutes space on your tape here. . .).

. . . *When you come to the plateau near the top of the mountain, there is a wonderful view over a large area of your inner landscape and a source of living water from which you can refresh yourself. . . . At one point the pathway leading from the plateau to the top of the mountain rounds a bend . . . be aware that the place where you will meet with the archetype of your choice, is a clear place just around that bend . . . there is no hurry . . . enjoy the plateau, the water, and the view first. . .*

. . . *At this point your power animal will lie down, as though on guard, and you will continue to the place where you will meet the archetype, your wise person, if accompanying you, may come to the archetype with you, but will stay at a distance while you make your dialogue with the archetype. . .*

. . . *Invoking the archetype of your choice, go now to the place where you will meet with this personification . . . spend a few*

75

moments just observing each other, but greet your archetype, and ask whether there is any comment to be made on the question which you have brought with you. . . . Say why you invoked this particular archetype at this time, and ask whether the archetype requires anything of you? has anything to give you? . . . Is there anything you require of the archetype, apart from comment on your question? (You have three minutes for this interaction . . . leave a space on your tape).

. . . It is time now to leave the archetype, and to return to the place where your power animal has been waiting for you. . . . Refresh yourself again from the source of living water if you wish to do so . . . take mental note that this place of refreshment is here in your inner space, and that you can come to this source of living water, life, and healing, any time when you have need . . . then with your wise being if he/she is present, and your talisman and any gifts you have received whilst making this journey, return to the meadow where you began. . . . You may return by the same route as you came, or by a different route. At some appropriate time you will part from the wise person and from your power animal, though they may accompany you to the meadow before taking their leave . . . gradually return from the meadow to a consciousness of your 'in-breath' and 'out-breath', and then to a full sense of your body relaxed on couch, chair or floor . . . lie for a few moments in the foetal position as you take in your everyday surroundings, and when you feel ready, perhaps having made a cup of tea or coffee record your journey in drawing or words, or both. . . .

From time to time, whenever you feel that there is an issue in your life that could be helped by comment from your inner wise person or from some other archetype this exercise can be repeated.

As you record, and think about the journey you made this time pay special attention to the nature of your inner wise being, your power animal, and the way in which the archetype of your choice personified for you.

The inner wise being was not referred to as either masculine or feminine, in order that you could find the figure which is right for you. It was designated as a 'being,' rather than a 'person'. Throughout this voyage through the inner worlds, the endeavour is to build up a picture of the whole guidance system, and its different levels. It is always good to trust the individual process in the psyche, thus the exercise description designated that there should be an inner wise being. The Psyche within the scope of that terminology will produce for you the being, person, or creature through which you may gain contact with your central core of wisdom.

The purpose in finding an inner wise being as well as a power animal was to bring experience of the different feeling which comes from an archetypal wise person or an energy being, (some people meet angelic or devic figures) and that which comes from a power animal. Later discussion related to chakras and using those energies to govern levels of experience may help clarity here. Within the pyschological framework of reference the differentiation may be seen as that which is instinctually wise (power animal), and that which is intuitively and to some extent mentally wise (wise being).

Similarly, for reasons which will be seen to be important later, stay with your own symbolism in the way of 'living alongside it'. See what it means to you, and how it works within you before attempting to move into areas of interpretation by reference to the sort of sources which may attempt to describe what it all 'means' in a too distancing, detached or intellectual way.

The next stage in self awareness, but also in discovery of areas and figures who give access to the inner guidance system, is the contacting of sub-personalities.

Many people who seek counselling and guidance are asking the basic question: 'Who am I?', and this is not such a strange question as it may seem. We are all multifaceted in the ways in which we express ourselves. We sense that in some way we are one person because we only have one physical body, but within, if we are given to any sort of introspection we know that we are neither simplistically made, nor unified.

On separate occasions, different motives, traits, attitudes, purposes and value systems may operate in us and in the way in which we handle life. In varying situations we may sense ourselves to be almost different personalities. Initial realization of this multifaceted quality of being sometimes brings anxiety, fear of loss of identity, of being a 'split personality', of going mad. Yet these aspects may belong to the inner parts of ourselves which were referred to by Jung as the 'persona' or 'mask', and seen by Assagioli to have almost separate existence as 'sub-personalities'. Such diverse identities are widely seen to be part of the normal range of experience and not belonging to abnormal pathology.

To some extent this multifaceted quality can be useful. It can be seen as a richness of our beings, and an opportunity for creativity. We do not necessarily *like* all our sub-personalities, however, and certainly in the early stages of self growth and self awareness they are not consciously under our control. We may suffer agonies of embarrassment or self criticism when a sub-personality asserts itself inappropriately. No wonder the question 'Who am I?' is heard so often by counsellors and psychotherapists. It is totally pertinent.

In the centre of the sub-personalities there is an 'I', which observes, makes judgements, is embarrassed, surprised, or pleased, sometimes seeming to experience all these things at one and the same time. It is this confusion, bewilderment or excitement which often brings the longing for guidance.

' *'I'* do not know what *'I'* want'; is a common feeling or complaint.

'One part of me says one thing, and another something different, it seems impossible to arrive at a decision'; is a well known statement.

Recognizing and becoming more aware of sub-personalities can help to give more certainty of that part which stands at the centre. Being in touch with the interplay between these different facets may bring respect for their needs and opinions. At the same time it can strengthen the knowledge of what the central 'I' truly wants. Contact with the sub-personalities means that decisions can be more effective, supported by strengths, and not unnecessarily undermined by unsuspected weaknesses. Access to the resources of the psyche, and compassion for its apparent weaknesses all becomes more conscious. The sub-personalities gradually become less dissociated or autonomous. The central 'I' becomes leader of a team, rather than surrounded by a bewildering array of non-communicating distinct universes.

Sub-personalities, experienced in the inner space manifest like characters in a drama, or perhaps more appropriately a circus. They can include animals, goblins, witches, clowns, mythological creatures, anything which can express a trait, attitude, need or motive. As they are recognized, there can be an experience of dismay or confrontation, because they do personify our weakness as well as our strengths. They often have needs of their own, having lived somewhat pathetically within for a long time, and will ask for nurturing, or opportunities for outlet in order that they may transform. They ask something then, in return for allowing a clearer answer to that question: 'Who am I?'

When first revealed the sub-personalities are not in general communication or awareness, the one of the other. There may be some partnerships or collusions, but on the whole they are distinct universes. Part of the task of integrating them is not only to identify and recognize them, not only to communicate with them from the central 'I', but to allow them to communicate with each other. In such communication they may fulfil some of each other's needs, though those which are at war may need to be helped to make peace. In the attention to all this work comes a deep sense of what true integration can mean.

When a sub-personality is given recognition, no matter how much from the shadow side of us it may seem to come, it begins to lose its autonomy. Our abilities to observe and discriminate, to understand or be compassionate can be activated towards it. Steps can be taken to be more in control of it, rather than being in its control.

Sub-personalities have been defined by Piero Ferrucci in his book 'What We May Be', as 'degraded expressions of the archetypes of higher qualities'. Related to this definition I would see many of them as the products of survival mechanisms within the psyche.

When recognizing sub-personalities most people will have an 'inner child' represented, and requiring to be nurtured. Negative as a whining, dirty, inner child may seem, sometimes it may have been necessary to retreat into such a sub-personality in order to be heard, or noticed. The inner child can also have very positive representation among the sub-personalities, as, for instance 'the magical child', keeping a sense of wonder, and anticipation alive within us.

Compulsively tidy, or bossy, or loud mouthed sub-personalities may have been at some time in life our only defence in a world seemingly falling apart, or without order. Often they are not aware that things are different now, and that therefore their exaggerated characteristics are no longer serving a purpose, but are merely taking energy from the psyche.

Some of the sub-personalities may have a wisdom of their own. It is arguable that the inner wise being is a sub-personality, perhaps nearer to one of the 'archetypes of higher qualities', but nevertheless a close relation of the sub-personalities. The inner wise being may already have seen the need to 'get on terms' with the sub-personality team, and be representative of the potential of the *Self,* in the Jungian sense, meaning the personality which has access to all its parts, in consciousness and at will.

In thinking about your attitudes, traits, motives, modes of behaviour at different times and in different situations, you may already have begun to recognize some of your own sub-personalities. If you think about these things in relationship to the 'stages of life' exercise, you may also see some of the circumstances which made particular sub-personalities evolve within you.

Working with sub-personalities in inner space helps them to transform. Such transformation may not be immediate but with patience, attention and inner dialogue all sorts of change and inner healing are possible.

It helps to give this inner team names, or designations, so that they can be recognized as they make their welcome or unwelcome appearance in your life. The aid of a sense of humour about your vulnerability to them is also very useful.

As work on self progresses, so the sub-personalities change, or even increase. There is, as in all things, a place for discretion, for sensing the optimum number of sub-personalities with which there can be positive work at any given time. Again the emphasis is on personal discrimination and responsibility. Trust the basic wisdom of your psyche, but have no inhibitions about calling a halt when 'enough is enough'.

Before proceeding to an exercise to help in identifying sub-personalities, describing some of my own, with whom I have found it valuable to work, may help.

Perhaps my most colourful sub-personality is a Spanish Dancer, complete with castanets and a rose in her teeth. She can be seductive and brash, and her taste is sometimes garish. Before I fully recognized and identified her she could certainly come out unexpectedly and act inappropriately. Since I have dialogued with her she helps my basic shyness, enables me to be more expressive with colour, and adds fun and sheer joie de vivre into my life.

In contrast to her, and gaining strength and help from her as the dialogue between my sub-personalities has developed is a very colourless, pathetic, almost cringing young person. This sub-personality I at first called 'The Cringer', but later changed her name to 'Daisy', because this reminds me of an evacuee I knew during ths war. She was white, and frightened, listless, and away from her environment. I felt a lot of compassion for her, and the name 'Daisy' has helped me to feel the same for this sub-personality. At first The Spanish Dancer would almost have ground her underfoot as she danced her flamenco, and 'Daisy' was terrified of her. Gradually they came to realise that there was ground for mutual exchange.

'Daisy' also received help from, and gave help to, a rather anguished mother with too many children, who has no name, but comes from the time of my life when I was entering teaching and not happy in it.

One of my favourites is The Free Spirit. She is more feminine than masculine, but fairly well balanced. She does not always relate well to the archetype of Responsibility, but on the other hand she refuses to be weighed down by the unimportant trivia of life.

I have probably said sufficient to give you the idea of the action and interaction. Just to balance up, because of course, women do not only have feminine sub-personalities and men masculine ones, I have, on the masculine side: an aggressive sports car driver; an efficient organizer, and a languid young man.

In this exercise to help you to meet with and recognize some of your sub-personalities, you will go to The River of Life, and there, at a place where there is a sort of natural harbour or back water, there will be a houseboat, firmly anchored on the river of life, and containing your sub-personalities. When you find this boat you do not go on board, but find yourself a pleasant place to sit in the sunshine whilst you invite, one by one, such of your sub-personalities as wish to reveal themselves at this time, to come out, just so that you can be more aware of them and they of you. At this stage you will not be dialoguing with them nor they with each other.

Prepare yourself for this exercise in the ways described elsewhere in this book. I give the instructions now, in such a way that they can be pre-recorded, or read to you by a friend or partner. The time required is about half an hour.

. . . *Find a place, lying out if you wish, in which you feel relaxed, warm, and comfortable. . . . Be in touch with the rhythm of of your breath, and let the focus of your breathing be in your heart centre, so that the energy of the heart is opened. . .*

. . . *Know that you are going into your inner space with the objectiive of meeting with and identifying your sub-personalities. You are going to begin the journey in the meadow, taking the opportunity there to awaken your inner senses of colour, sound, fragrance, smell and taste. . . . Ask whether there is an appropriate talisman to take with you on this journey, or see whether you are already carrying a familiar one. . .*

. . . *There is a pathway which leads from the meadow to the River of Life. Take that pathway, and spend the next three minutes journeying to that part of the River of Life, where in a safe natural harbour or backwater, there is a houseboat where your sub-personalities live. . . .* (Leave a three minute space on your tape. . .).

. . . *As you find the place where the house boat containing your sub-personalities is anchored, take note of the place, and of the condition of the boat and the immediate envronment . . . then find a space where you feel at ease, with the sun shining warmly upon you, and perhaps with your back against a tree . . . sense the presence of your talisman, and invoke the presence of your inner wise Being if you feel that you need company at this point. . .*

. . . *When you are ready let it be known that you invite your sub-personalities to come out of the houseboat, one at a time, unless there is amongst them an inseperable pair. . . . Remember that they may be people, animals, mythological creatures, any-*

*thing which gives them shape or identity ... the suggestion is
that you should, at this point, meet with no more than six of these
sub-personalities revealing themselves one at a time ... but the
final decision is yours. ... Make sure that each personality either
retreats to a distance, or returns to the houseboat respecting your
right to meet the team one at a time. ... If this does not happen,
ask all sub-personalities to return to the boat, and you return to
the meadow, with the intent of trying the exercise at some other
time. ... You now have ten minutes in which to meet the
appropriate sub-personalities for this time, to recognize them and
acknowledge them without dialoguing with them. ...* (Leave a
ten minute space on your tape. . .).

*... It is time now to thank the sub-personalities who have
revealed themselves, and to let them know, if you can make some
sort of commitment at this stage, that they will no longer be
neglected, and that you intend to work with them. ... They will
all now return to the houseboat, and you return to the meadow,
and from the meadow to the consciousness of your breath in your
heart centre ... your body on the chair, couch or floor, and your
everyday surroundings ... lie for a short while in the foetal
position as you absorb this experience, and then record in
drawing, if possible, and also writing, the details of the meeting
with these sub-personalities. . .*

Just being aware of the sub-personality mechanism in
yourself can gradually bring about transformations in your
life. I am not here going to give specific further exercises
for working in this area, there are a number of sources (See
Bibliography) where you may find these. Much of the
work to be done with sub-personalities is on the psychological level, and I have endeavoured to show how important this level of growth is to sound guidance work. I
consider dialoguing with inner figures to be part of what I
have termed the inner guidance system.

When you are seeking guidance, it can help to be 'on
terms' with your sub-personalities, because their thoughts
and reactions to various topics or necessary decisions can
throw considerable light in understanding the choice of
your inner majority, or in discovering where you are
blocked, or held back in your decision making.

Let me re-emphasise too, that the way to transparency lies in
knowing where autonomous sub-personalities may be colouring your view of the world, and in dealing with that autonomy.

Though I am not going on in a formal way with the exploration of the characters who live in the houseboat, I do suggest that you take seriously the need to dialogue with, and continue to recognize interactions between them, and that you do this in a way which is specifically related to the inner guidance theme. Thus, as you record your impressions of this first meeting with your sub-personalities think which ones would either like to dialogue with each other or need to dialogue with each other in order to achieve better inner harmony and communication. See which ones are related to strengths which can specifically be of use in your life, and think about harnessing those strengths.

Consider your inner landscape, and The River of Life, with the place with the houseboat where you met your sub-personalities. Think of the way in which your inner wise being may be able to help you to bring harmony and transformation to this inner team. Decide on a place in your landscape, or the place near the houseboat, and from time to time invite one or more of the personalities you have met, to join you there for dialogue and interaction.

Remember that the more you bring something which may carry aspects you dislike in yourself into consciousness, the more is there opportunity for transformation. Above all remember that you are in charge of the pace, and if that ever seems in doubt seek some help from the sources already mentioned.*

In the exercise there was a very specific instruction that unless the sub-personalities respected your right to meet them separately you should in effect close the interview. This instruction was in order to emphasise all that I have written in the last paragraph. There is no doubt that in inner space you can meet with parts of yourself or aspects of living which you dislike or find threatening. Methods of psychic protection will be discussed later, but usually unless you are pushing too hard, trying to progress too fast, not respecting the rhythms and meaningful defences of the psyche, the way is safe, and exciting and leads to fuller and deeper effectiveness in living

Be creative with your sub-personalities, and compas-

* See page 17.

sionate, see their humour, and their pathos, and you will help them to reunite with the pure essence of the archetypes of higher qualities. Eventually you may actually ask each one the final question you may have found in the 'questions exercise', the answer you gave to 'What question should I be asking now?' The differing or similar answers which the sub-personalities may give, could help further in depth and breadth of self understanding.

In the next chapter the consideration moves on more specifically to discarnate guidance, and some of Gildas' teaching on this.

CHAPTER 4

Approaching Discarnate Guidance

The inner guidance system has been the main substance of consideration until this point, with some discussion on levels, and possible areas or other planes from which guidance if discarnate comes.

My definition of discarnate guidance is that guidance which comes from another distinct entity, who is not a symbolic or representative figure *within* the individual psyche nor a personification of an archetype.

Coming into the world of discarnate guidance there is, even in discussion, a passage through the interface which lies between the world of psychology, understood in its absolute and most universally accepted sense, into the world of esoteric spiritual exploration. As stated in the first chapter terms may be similar, but shades of meaning and the structure of this spiritual area are often different. It is my particular interest to endeavour fully to open up this interface, and reinforce both areas of experience by making comprehensible connections from the one to the other, and by emphasising the way in which, in my view, for true growth, and strength to function in the world, both areas must be embraced.

Discarnate guidance may open up and be experienced before any psychological growth or insight has been set in motion. In this event the next wise step is to seek to know oneself psychologically, and to seek the resources of the inner guidance system in helping to have clearer receptivity, clarity and discrimination about discarnate guidance.

Discarnate guidance is becoming a 'fashion', and even a 'cult' in these times and the pitfalls are many and often deep. The 'New Age' movement is too often used as a means by which individuals so sensitize themselves that they can no longer live comfortably in the world as we know it. Their energies become completely focussed on making their own environment stress free with the result that they cannot be effective in outer living. I do not consider that this state should be the result of spiritual growth and training. Those who focus on their spiritual strengths can become more adequate in the outer world, and able to work there with the view to expressing spiritual values such as love and integrity to combat disillusionment, corruption and cold self-interested competition. Fortunately there is a breed of such people emerging, who believe in, and work for the coming of the 'New Age', but who are beginning to shudder at the way in which this term has become so unfortunately loaded with all sorts of other connotations.

In my experience the true discarnate guides are seeking to help individuals, races, humanity, to heal themselves and the earth; to bring spirit into matter without rejecting matter or condemning technological advances out of hand. It is possible in every sense to live in harmony with mind, body, emotions and spirit, and this means giving value, equality and joy to each mode of expression. When all functions are honoured humanity will no longer be *able* to create that which is out of balance with the needs of the substance of earth itself. There can be an end to that which is disharmonious, twisted, ugly or unfair in the behaviour of one human being to another, or of group to group and nation to nation.

The true discarnate guides, as I have experienced them, do not seek to lead away from the things of earth in the sense of true concern for life and the planet, not to inflate the individual by giving the message that guidance and access to the discarnate worlds cancels out the need for psychological growth. Rather do they seek to give support in and through that growth process, bringing to it an added dimension of deeper meaning in its significance and necessity.

Who, or what are they then, these discarnate figures who are neither personifications of the inner processes of the psyche nor of archetypes? In order to explain *themselves* they give us a cosmology which goes beyond the world of the individual psyche and the collective consciousness of humanity. They take us beyond the concept of one life span into embracing the evolution of souls, and the incarnation of the soul essence into many personalities throughout time and history in order to build experience for that soul evolution. Namely they speak to us of reincarnation.

In this way Gildas, (my discarnate guide), can say that his last incarnation was as a Benedictine monk in the fourteenth century in France, since which time he has continued his evolution on another plane of existence, unbound by the same dimensions of time and space as earth incarnation. He is not an angelic being, he is of the human stream of consciousness travelling towards reunion with the Ultimate Source. He speaks of groups of discarnates working in various ways to help humanity, the planet earth, and the raising of consciousness. Their work is accomplished in various ways according to the group to which they are attached. Some, like Gildas are concerned with contacting and teaching humanity about the positive relationship which can exist between these planes of consciousness, and the ways in which that relationship could help us in our personal and collective lives.

Almost all seem to have an interest in healing in the broadest sense in which that term may be understood. Others work to bring through inspiration as to architecture, design, music, sound, colour, literature and art. Yet others seem to be intent on working with the etheric or higher levels of these aspects, including the nature of light, to form structures and temples which hold power and harmony of consciousness for us until such time as it is able to manifest more thoroughly on the earth plane.

There would seem to be an immense organization on these other planes. They are, of course the planes to which we begin to have access when we pass through the experience of death. One of the most reiterated messages is that death is an initiation and that life continues, and that when we truly release our fear of death it will be easier for us to live incarnate life from a different perspective. Groups of discarnate beings who work with healing are there on the other side to receive those who pass through death, and to help them to understand and find the best place, after healing and re-orientation, in which to continue the journey of consciousness.

Even more than in life, many choices are possible to arrivals into this other dimension or plane of consciousness. Development and evolution continue, there is not instant access to wisdom, or openness to it. Many who arrive on the other planes continue to be worried about their loved one on earth, and to seek to contact them either to reassure them, or because various energies of unworked out pieces of relationship remain active. This leads to a fascination with the earth plane so recently left, and the new dimension in which it is seen from that place in which time and space are so different.

Apparently some beings are not content to give reassuring messages to loved ones, or to clear up 'unfinished business' in a dignified way, or acknowledge when it must be *left* unfinished. The 'other side' is not a place where responsbility is taken away, help, guidance and healing are available but gentle angels or wise discarnate beings do not direct one explicitly to a 'divine' area of service. Free will still operates. With so many potentialities this can lead into discarnate activity of a questionable nature, often coloured by the degree to which there has, or has not been awareness of the need for positive growth whilst in incarnation.

This means then, that it is possible, once one opens up the veil to contact with beings on other planes, to have dialogue with entities who are not wiser, or more advanced, or more detached in their perspective just because they are discarnate.

How increasingly clear it becomes that these levels need to be contacted with all that is wisest, and most integrated within us at a personality level, strongly in consciousness! I am often asked the question: 'Can the level of discarnate which is being contacted be differentiated, or even governed in advance?' Gildas teaches, and I believe, that it can. It must therefore increasingly be explored with will and consciousness and not just by chance encounter when relatively or completely unprepared.

It has been well said, that there can be too much concern about the nature and identity of the source of guidance, a statement which Gildas has often reiterated. What comes should be judged by its quality, and by the manner in which it speaks to the individual. If it brings a sense of insight which was being sought, but just missed, if it awakens a sense of inner sureness and connectedness; a pure surge of creativity; a sense of being able to breathe again; clarity as to the next step to take, or any response which is recognized as coming truly from the heart of our beings, then it is of no account to substantiate the authority by being too intent on the exact nature of the source.

I am aware that there are paradoxes in this statement. Much of my thesis has been about knowing your inner territory, distinguishing where you are, to whom you are speaking, knowing the way there in order to know the way back etc. This *is* of extreme importance in recognizing the different areas of reality, and in being able to expand the narrow models of reality from which we are all too often living. It is necessary in order to build up confidence to be able to go to other levels, heights, or depths without losing touch with the physical, valuable and demanding reality in which we communally and objectively live. Yet when the level of guidance or inner voice or perspective is touched which makes the heart beat in response, and the whole of life sing, it is an acknowledgement of potential to which there is access. In order to contact it again there may be a certain sequence to be followed, certain conducive outer conditions to bring into being, but when *such* a voice has spoken, *does* it matter whether it is a sub-personality, an inner wise being, a power animal or archetype, or Gildas – a discarnate being whose last incarnation was in fourteenth century France?

The answer to this question in principle is 'No'. When guidance is experienced we are moved by it, and respond to it with that within us which is other than pure rationality, and yet supports and can be supported by the rational too. It is the experience of being 'on truth', or 'on centre'.

Nevertheless in the world of inner guidance, if training has been careful, and observation sharpened discrimination becomes growingly acute. The very format, intent and invocation by which the work is done, the structure which is brought to it, the self responsibility which is taken, will usually bring at least some sense of which inner aspect it is that speaks the guidance to which there is response at any given moment.

There are greater problems with dicarnate guidance. When the discarnate world is contacted there is a new shift of consciousness. Suddenly there is an awareness of a different sense of tension, and if a figure is present it is something like realizing that one has spoken an inner thought aloud without being aware of, or forgetting about the presence of another person in the room. There is a surge of excitement and fascination, perhaps even nervousness or fear. Suddenly one's hypotheses about other worlds, life on other planes, the continuity of life look like being confirmed. That very possibility of confirmation is like a confrontation. Carefully learned discrimination from and for the other levels may suddenly seem inaccessible. One can watch, look, listen or flee, except that there may also be an almost mesmeric quality to this contact. If one chooses to flee, – where to? Again, in all these instances, the value of carefully getting to know the inner planes, in order not only to gain access to discarnate guidance, but to maintain integrity when that access comes, can be seen. Knowing the inner planes, having trained carefully through other exercises, if flight is the choice, there are known places to which to go, known inner strengths on which to call. Stature and dignity can be maintained, the right sort of questions can be asked with satisfactory answers demanded.

All these experiences work together to make it possible, if the right discarnate is present, to be able to move on towards developing a creative contact with that discarnate.

As has been discussed, however, there is no guarantee that the discarnate we come into contact with in such a way carries the particular quality of wisdom which is being sought. In the inner worlds it has been seen that invocation and intent, together with an openness to the creative power and wisdom of the psyche will lead to where we wish to go, or to the approximate area. The aspect to be met with has been previously determined. Its form may be a surprise, but it will usually be recognisable to us. In the early stages at least of encountering the discarnate worlds there is much more openness, and even a searching which may hold something of the rather hackneyed question, 'Is there anybody there?' attached to it.

The identity of the source, the level of the source, whilst not exactly needing to be asked to present its credentials does need sober consideration. The interests of self protection and proof against early disillusionment depend upon it. The option of flight, or the composure and dignity to stand one's ground and ask the right questions go a long way. But not far enough.

'Quality' has been mentioned as being necessary to evaluation rather than the identity of the source. If quality has been touched, and discrimination holds then indeed it does not signify whether the words come from within the field of inner guidance, from a discarnate source or from a meaningful book picked up through synchronicity. Unfortunately it is not always so simple in practice. Ascertaining the level of the source, at least to one's own inner standard of satisfaction is *very* important.

'It does not help', a friend in some difficulty with the discarnate worlds once said to Gildas, 'to be told that quality of communication is the chief standard by which to judge. It takes at least half a page of dictation, or some time in the presence of another entity in order to judge their quality or integrity. I feel resentful that I have been obliged to be in that presence, for that length of time when I eventually distinguish that the communicating entity is incompatible, or the teaching and level of concept unacceptable.' He went on to ask Gildas for ways of verifying as soon as possible that the discarnate with whom one is in contact is intent upon sound guidance and the 'higher good'.

As part of a long answer about discarnate guidance Gildas spoke as follows:

'I do appreciate your difficulty, and there are many factors involved in this question of differentiation, many more precise definitions as to factors involved in the process, which need to be made.

The first requirement is increased sensitivity, and this does not necessarily carry the esoteric mystique which is often associated with it. It is basically a sensitized capacity for observation which carries both the quality of diffuseness *and* focussed alertness. Within the definition of 'increased', lies the openness and imagination to set aside the forms, expectations and limitation of outer perception, in order to know the subtleties and nuances of inner perception. This means basically releasing the expectation that inner vision, hearing, and the other senses are experienced in exactly the same way as the outer senses. In some ways inner perception is more vivid, in others it is more subtle. Skill in registering it depends upon realizing that perception is complex in general, and in the inner worlds diffuse. This skill also depends on the focussed alertness which guards against the seduction which that very diffuseness can have. Thus the observer, with the qualities of registration and discrimination must be kept fully engaged.

This already begins to give some proof against being 'sucked in' to an experience, before the necessary period for 'the testing of the spirits' has been observed. No discarnate who is of pure intent will invade your being. In the extra dimensions of our perceptions and knowledge we recognize that we have to observe the strictest integrity about the sacred and private psychic space around an individual. Also the area of free will. Our own space is also very sensitive, and there has to be an initial period of 'sensing out' the other for all parties concerned.

This means that no benign discarnate entity will approach too suddenly, or will object to space for mutual scrutiny. The sort of observation which goes on in that space carries several key words which may be of use to you from your side of the encounter. The first of these key words must be the same one which mainly prompted your question. That is the key word of 'quality'. Here, though, I use quality in a different context from the quality of content. I use it to describe the quality of being, the quality of feeling, the quality of respect, and in relationship to being able to evaluate from some of the other key words which I shall use.

The second key word, which should be put along-side quality, is 'fragrance'. This refers to more than the olefactory sense of fragrance. It is an experience which I hope you may have known in your ordinary everyday contacts or relationships. That essence of the space around a person which gives a definite sense of wanting to draw nearer to that person, much as one wants to draw nearer to the fragrance of a beautiful flower. With heightened perception then, inextricably linked to focussed observation, sense the fragrance of the one who draws near to you in the discarnate world, or who invites you to draw near. If that fragrance causes your heart and being to open without fear, then approach, if you wish, or be approached more closely. All true discarnate guides will give you the choice of movement, it is for you to approach, or retreat. Remember your own responsibility to your own psychic space too, do not allow yourself to be invaded.

The next key word is similar in some respects to fragrance, it is the key word of 'texture'. Be aware of the quality of the texture of anyone who approaches you. Does the emanence around the presence seem harsh, or abrasive?, or is there a gentleness, a smoothness there, which allows any apprehensions you have about this sort of experience you are involved in to gradually subside? Again, take time, test it out, how does it feel? do not go further until you are satisfied as to texture.

After texture comes vibration. It is linked to sound, to light, and to speed. As discarnates we have different levels of vibration from those which you have on earth. Though you may not be fully conscious of it, it will probably have been vibration in the first place which led you to sense that the being you have met is from another plane, and not from the inner world of psychological and transpersonal experience. The true communicators from these other planes have a very finely attuned vibration, and will seek to help you to raise your own vibrational rate, in order to be comfortable in the meeting. In practice, at a vibrational level we would find it very difficult to invade you, often we cannot reach you, because you are not into the inner experience at the right vibrational rate for us to be able to link in with you. So raising your vibrational level in order to enter, or to seek entry into the world of discarnate presence, is also a very useful safeguard for you, and I will say more of this later. As I have urged you to do then with the other key word aspects, sense the quality of the vibration which emanates from the presence. Observe it, assess it, and if it is uncomfortable sense again whether you are being gently helped to meet that vibration, or whether there is any element of disregard, and therefore of invasion. The vibration of a true guide, is a vibration of unconditional love and positive regard, with often a touch of gentle humour.

The final key word which I wish to give you to reflect upon in this context for the moment is the key word of 'frequency'. I have said that vibration is concerned with the *level* of contact, and this is even more directly true with frequency. When a radio is attuned, in your world to the correct frequency, there is a quality of reception which is clear and without interference. The true guide will patiently await, and patiently help the process of attunement. Those discarnates who seek contact more for their own purposes will often be content with imperfect attunement, a sense of 'buzz', which is again in the region of invasion. Assess the quality of attunement, whether the frequencies are in alignment, in order to allow the message to be clear, and the experience an energizing one. A radio which is 'off frequency' can be very de-energizing. Your true friends from the discarnate worlds seek to bring you energy, and not depletion. I am aware that in what I have said there are things which need amplification. Reflect on what has passed between us, and try to frame the questions which will most help me to be of assistance to you in these important areas of experience and investigation. My love and blessing are with you.'

It was largely on the basis of this teaching that I asked Gildas' help in developing the sensitivity, and sense exercises given in Chapter 1. Their relevance may now be seen in the context of discarnate guidance.

There has been much mention of the word 'quality', and Gildas has attempted to give his definitions as to the way in which to sense the quality of those aspects covered by his key words. Assessing the quality of a message which has been received needs more discussion.

Gildas has affirmed that our true guides are unconditionally loving and compassionate. They may have to take a dispassionate role in some aspects of our training and self discovery if we decide to work with them,* but the note of their teaching always contains congruence, and infinite patience and understanding. Guidance is present without over direction or control. It is clear where the ultimate responsibility as to choice lies, and also that whatever decision you make will be supported and helped in that decision with respect. The vision of a wider perspective is offered with that detachment which is without indifference. The experience of the communication is often confirming, or lifting, one feels valued and truly seen. Even actions of which one is ashamed are accepted and put into the context of experience. Release of guilt is encouraged and one is given courage to go forward to the next step in life. There is no sense that toil and grind and unpleasantness are the only ways of learning. Compassion for our sorrows is there, but the message is that we can step forward into joy or sunshine just as soon as we can release ourselves from some of the burdens which we seem to insist on carrying.

By contrast there are communicatons which are extremely directive, peremptory and forceful. Often they carry a sense of urgency or of immediate expectation that some relatively inconvenient task or move will be undertaken at the express directive of the voice or presence. Insufficient explanation or support is given, there is an atmosphere of 'I/We know best, stop asking so many time consuming questions'. So, I have known someone be told, 'The whole of your life has been a series of mistakes. Arrange to go to Australia as soon as possible and start again.' The understandable questions arising from this directive met with no helpful response, just a reiteration in a tone which buzzed with increasing irritation and anger, 'I have spoken, go to Australia, you will be given more directions there'.

It seems that some discarnates enjoy sending people from one place to another, for flimsy reasons, or to make 'contacts'. The power of the discarnate voice, the experience of the discarnate presence can be such that even

* See 'Seven Inner Journeys' Ruth White and Mary Swainson pub. C. W. Daniel.

normally level headed people lose their 'distancing' and discrimination, and rush to obey. Great anxiety can be suffered if the practical barriers to following such advice seem insurmountable.

Such 'messengers' are often inflationary, both of themselves and of those to whom they speak. Thus the 'I have spoken . . .' states implicitly 'do not question my authority'. The 'reward' for following instructions may be promised as wealth, or fame, or great powers of healing. The distinction must be made between this sort of inflation, and the gentle support and encouragement to self worth which comes from the true guide. They neither seek to assert their authority, inflate themselves nor to take away the authority and right of choice of the individuals they wish to help.

A sort of 'jealousy' is another aspect which is exhibited by those discarnates whom I can only really eventually title as 'false guides'. This is often exhibited towards concern with which one is involved in the outer world, or relationships one holds dear. 'X is not a good influence on you, he/she keeps you away from your true work'. 'Cancel this weekend's outing, I have other things for you to do'. These sort of messages can come if one has been unwise enough to go on soliciting contact with a discarnate whose quality does not stand up to close scrutiny.

There can be uncomfortable nuances to such statements as: 'Do what I say and you will become a great healer'. We can all be susceptible to flattery, and also hopeful that as a 'great healer' many people could be helped. If such a statement is rejected on the grounds of its being over directive, imperative and inflating, guilt, questioning and depression can result.

Yet the answer to such a dilemma is clear. If you have healing ability the best means of developing it are through your own self-knowledge, sensitivity and awareness. Discarnate *support* could be very helpful, but it must be support without that threatening tone. Return to simple logic and know that the ability to help others will not be taken away because of lack of faith in a discarnate, whether the guide be true *or* false. Even so the inner questioning coming from such encounters can be very uncomfortable and unsettling.

Are these 'false guides' then evil, or merely mischievous? Some of them seem to be trying out a sense of power without taking into account the consequences for those whom they seek to move around or confuse. Some may be genuinely endeavouring to help, but this is the time to remember that 'discarnate' is not synonymous with 'evolved'. The perspective being offered may be less than that to which your own inner wise part has access.

Other discarnates, it must categorically be said, are not of 'good report'. I do not necessarily hold a dualistic* view of the universe. In the incarnate world however, there are individuals who manipulate power for selfish and sometimes evil ends. It seems naive to expect that crossing to another plane of existence will immediately and automatically change such individuals.

Again, the thought of other planes, and beings who reside there, and have a different perspective from our own, is a powerful one. Authority is easily given to those who speak from that dimension. Within ourselves we hold expectations and fears of how 'authority' should, or does speak, and what our reaction to that 'should' be. Some peremptoriness then from other planes may be our own colouring of expectation. It is as easy to hear that which comes from our negative projections as it is to hear that which comes from our positive projections. Making all this conscious means that guidance can be interpreted. It is possible to be sensitive to the likely areas of colouring, and not 'throw out the baby with the bathwater'.

These things are not included here with intent to frighten. Part of the excitement and stimulus of the journey is that one 'needs to be on one's metal'. It is not a journey for the faint hearted. Another assumption which I often hear is: 'I'll be all right because my true guides and guardian angels will protect me.' I believe absolutely that we all have guides and guardian angels. They can and do protect us to a remarkable extent, but there come moments when it is no longer appropriate for them to protect ourselves from ourselves. We are not children, and even children must learn from experience. If no regard is given to discovering the ground rules, or to training for

* *dualistic: belief in opposing powers of good and evil.*

the ascent or journey, possibility of trouble is invited. Our guides and helpers may be able to modify that trouble for us. Often they seem to walk beside us, on the outside, as we insist on traversing the precipices ill-prepared. Sometimes they have to stand at a distance whilst mistakes are made and can do no more than send light and love, and help to see that we are 'picked up' and put on our way again. The word 'responsibility', meaning *self* responsibility recurs with what some consider to be boring frequency in the exploration of inner and discarnate worlds. The experience of guidance never can be a way to find all pathways smooth, all decisions easy. It is a way to cooperation, and to finding loving supportive companionship from another dimension.

For all these reasons any risks or disciplines of training which need to be undertaken are more than worthwhile. There is that inherent within us which knows that this quality of contact with other planes is possible. Why otherwise do so many enter the search? If we stay true to that inner knowledge, and some sense of self evaluation, we shall not easily be deluded into settling for that which is inferior.

CHAPTER 5

About Chakras and their Relationship to Levels of Guidance

Beyond, but also as part of the search for quality of guidance come considerations as to the level of guidance. In one sense the word level in this context might seem very similar to quality. In another sense it carries the weight of yet another perspective and dimension for training and awareness. There is often confusion concerning that which is psychic and that which is spiritual. 'Psychic' has a specific meaning and intent when used purely in the psychological sense, and a rather different connotation when used in the language of esoteric spiritual exploration.

In the first chapter there was discussion of this difference, and I recap on it now as a point of reference. In psychology the whole experiencing part of the being is spoken of as 'the psyche'. The different energies which operate psychologically within us are the 'energies of the psyche', different areas of experience within the psyche then become 'areas of the psyche', or 'realms of the psyche'. Confusion arises when the phrases mentioned are shortened to 'psychic energies' or 'psychic realms or areas'.

In the world of esoteric spiritual exploration, the term 'psychic' is usually used to denote people who have very sensitive, or open auras, and who therefore easily cross the normal boundaries of perception. The term 'psychic phenomena' does not denote that which happens within the individual psyche, but that which happens beyond the normal range of experience. It most usually describes seemingly autonomous energies and happenings such as poltergeist experiences when solid objects are moved by scientifically unexplainable forces.

Psyche, as defined by the Oxford Dictionary is 'soul, spirit; mind.' Psychology, and esoteric spiritual exploration are concerned with the inter-personal, and intra-personal workings and definitions of these intangible areas of experience, though often approaching them from different angles of perception. It can eventually make things clearer, though at first seeming to add complexity to realize that there is this other interface between psychic and spiritual. In my view it is essential to be aware of it, and to attempt to define it, that there may be greater acuity in assessing 'quality' and 'level' in discarnate contact and guidance.

My definition of psychic would be that it can be concerned with mediumship, discarnate guidance, divination and fortune telling if these things are linked to the lower will rather than to the higher will. When information is sought only to clarify matters on a mundane level, then it will often have a mundane limitation. We tend to get what we ask for, hence the importance of understanding the significance of invocation and intent. The lower will is linked to the personality, that part which is represented by the dot in the centre of the Assagioli Egg Map, the little ego. The higher will is linked to the sun self, and to the soul. Seeking the sort of guidance which will help to link the personality to the soul and vice versa, and to understand the purposes of the soul for this incarnation will tend to lift the guidance to a less limited level.

Certain sorts of 'fortune telling' or divination may sometimes be seen as linked more to the psychic than the spiritual. Tarot cards, palmistry, crystal ball reading, even astrology are sometimes seen in this way. Yet it is not the instrument being used, but the level of the purpose in using it, and in interpreting it which is important. It is reassuring to see Tarot and astrology particularly, being used more and more now for helping to link to purpose, and direction rather than to sheer curiosity about the future and specific relationship expectations. Thus many practitioners are lifting these arts from the psychic to the spiritual within my definition.

In chakra terms the lower will is related to the solar plexus, the higher will to the crown and the brow. When there is an understanding then, of chakra energies, it becomes more possible to gather and direct the intent towards the levels most related to spiritual and soul purpose. For this reason I will give now a brief introduction to the chakras. The statements made are based on teaching which Gildas has given. Other interpretations and other systems exist. These do not necessarily contradict each other. It is always the angle of perception which needs to be considered.

The word chakra comes from Sanskrit and means 'wheel'. Properly speaking the singular is chakrum, but the generally accepted terminology in the West is to speak of one chakra, and several chakras.

When sensitives, clairvoyants, healers, and advanced yogis, look at the human being, they may see a subtle energy field around that being which is called the aura. It is often seen in colour, and can give quite a lot of information in terms of health, happiness, potential, or present state of mind. The chakras are part of this energy field. They are seen clairvoyantly as pulsating, rotating wheels of light at seven or eight major points in the body. There are many minor chakras but the main system is seen in alignment down the body, from the crown of the head to where the trunk of the body joins the legs. The auric space extends to between four to six inches around the physical body. The chakras extend out at front and back into this space. Their energy field also interpenetrates the physical body and interacts with the physical, emotional, mental, and spiritual functioning.

Some sources give a seven point major chakra system, others eight. Gildas always refers to eight major chakras, and has recently suggested that part of the work of the Aquarian Age is to awaken four other major chakras. This teaching will form the substance of another book. For the purposes of using levels of awareness in guidance eight chakras will suffice! These are: (See diagram D p 103 for help in positioning them). the crown, the brow, the alter major, the throat, the heart, the solar plexus, the sacral centre, and the root. When they are seen, there is an effect of pulsating and rotating petals at the front of the body, and of a closed stem effect at the back. The petals can open and close, thus opening up sensitivity and perception, or keeping it gently closed when it is appropriate to do so.

Diagram D

Positions of the chakra 'petals' and the 'central column' which interpenetrates the physical body

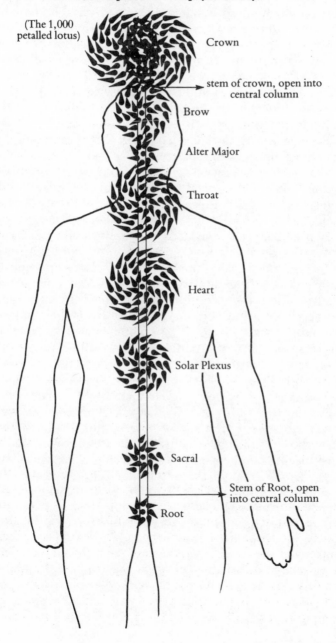

(The 1,000 petalled lotus)

Crown

stem of crown, open into central column

Brow

Alter Major

Throat

Heart

Solar Plexus

Sacral

Stem of Root, open into central column

Root

A healthy chakra is a flexible chakra. The chakras are in alignment. This enables energy to pass through the whole system by means of a central channel or column of subtle energy which interpenetrates with the physical body. This central column runs through the physical body, and the centre of the chakras where they permeate the body horizontally. It runs from the crown to the root, allowing energies to be drawn up and down the body, in at the crown, and out through the root, and vice versa. Energies are also drawn in to the being and sent out through the individual chakra petals. (See diagram on page 103).

Each chakra vibrates in such a way that it carries one of the colour notes of the spectrum. The root chakra has the lowest rate of vibration and its colour note is red; the colour note of the sacral is orange; of the solar plexus yellow; of the heart green; of the throat blue; of the alter major brown ochre; of the brow indigo, and of the crown violet. By colour note, it is meant that a particular chakra is responsible for that colour in the aura and being of the individual. Any, or every colour can be appropriate in any chakra, together with its own colour note. Auric interpretations often rely on 'reading' the different colours in the chakras and deriving meaning from their placing and interaction. Although all colours may appear in all chakras, each chakra producing a good colour of its own note gives indication of physical, mental, emotional, and spiritual health, vitality, and balance.

The rate of vibration of each chakra affects the way in which it is clairvoyantly perceived. The chakras with lower vibrational rates appear more simple, less complex than those with higher vibrational rates. Some sources give specific numbers of petals for each chakra, the crown thus becoming the 'thousand petalled lotus', and the root chakra having four petals. I often see the chakras quite clearly when attuned for giving healing, not with specific clarity as to the number of petals, but rather a sense of increasing complexity and vibration in moving up the scale.

As well as colours the chakras are linked to elements, and the five lower ones and the alter major* to physical

* The word 'alter' is often spelt 'alta', particularly in the writings of Alice Bailey. Gildas has asked for the former spelling to denote the meaning 'other'.

senses. Thus the root is linked to the element of earth and the sense of smell; the sacral to water and taste; the solar plexus to fire and sight; the heart to air and touch; the throat to hearing and ether; the alter major to wet earth and smell. The brow is linked to the spirit, and the element of radium. The crown is the bridge to the soul, and is given the element of magnetum. These last two elements and their significance have not yet been fully described by Gildas, the chakras are the main currrent area of his teaching.

Although it is necessary to speak of lower and higher chakras and lower and higher rates of vibration, the term 'lower' does not denote inferior in quality. It either relates to the position of the chakra in the body of an upright being, or vibrationally, to a lower note in the scale, without which the scale could not be complete. The terms higher and lower have come to carry evaluatory weight, or to refer to hierarchical systems. In understanding the use of the chakras in enabling spiritual exploration, and contact with discarnate guidance, it is essential to see them as a team, and to use all the energies appropriately.

To work only from the lower chakras brings serious limitation in vision. Working only from the upper chakras can bring limitation of incarnate experience, and splitting from, or guilt about areas governed by the lower chakras.

Before considering how each chakra energy can be employed in the search for specific levels and quality of guidance, I will expand further on the characteristics governing, and governed by, each chakra.

The root, with its colour red, element of earth and sense of smell, is also a chakra of instinct and incarnation. Thus, being born into the world, we come with instinctual needs for food, warmth, shelter, closeness, and love. If these needs are met the root chakra will have positive strength, and there will be a good relationship to the things of earth. They will be neither under or over valued, but there will be ability to relate well to the worlds and its requirements.

A well developed root chakra also means the ability to take responsibility for self nurturing. Dependence on parents or parent substitute figures comes to a happily resolved end. There is no need either for aggressive over assertion or independence.

The physical situation of the root chakra is near the sex organs, but it is only concerned with sexuality to the extent that sex is an instinct, and to the extent that a good relationship to the things of earth gives positive grounding for the development of sexuality.

The sacral chakra, with orange as its colour, water as its element and taste as its sense, is the centre of vitality and creativity, and of conscious sexuality. It is linked to the emotions, as they are experienced in the first rather raw state. When it is harmoniously developed it becomes a chakra of empowerment and enables an empathic sense of others and the quality of sincerity. Its relationship to the sense of taste should be seen in all aspects of the meaning of that word. Hence taste in fashion, and attitudes, trends and cults are partly governed by the sacral centre.

The solar plexus links to the colour yellow, the element of fire, and the sense of light. It is the centre of the 'little ego', or the personality and the lower will. The fire element conects with assimilation both of actual food, and of the symbolic food of knowledge, and discovery. The solar plexus is a particularly energized centre and thus attracts other energies in accordance with the laws of physics. In its connection to sight lies the link to its function as a centre of psychism, clairvoyance, and psychic phenomena. This centre is particularly active in growing children aged eight to twelve years. It has been found that where there are potentially psychically and spiritually sensitive children of this age in a household there may be a link with the occurrence of psychic phenomena. This is the age range where the 'spoon bending' abilities which have attracted attention in recent years also tend to develop.

The solar plexus is a complex centre, and can further be seen as the 'shock absorber' of the being. It responds to atmospheres, and incidents, often before there has been a chance to take them in at a rational level. Thus when it is particularly sensitized it can help in giving access to information which transcends the boundaries of time and space. The premonition, or deja vu experience are usually solar plexus linked. In this way it can be seen that it is a very useful and valuable member of the team in accessing the energies which lead to the expansion of the normal boundaries of experience. The fire element, too is linked to the flow of intuition. If it is spiritual experience you are seeking it is necessary to take the energy of the solar plexus beyond its own level, but it has primary input into the capacities to experience other worlds, and the development of intuition. Working only from the level of the solar plexus will tend to limit experience to the psychic, (as here defined). Without harnessing solar plexus energy spiritual vision and experience can be limited, and certainly ungrounded.

The heart has green as it colour, air as its element and touch as its sense. Touch needs to be understood widely, so that it links fully into feeling. It is the ability to touch, and to be touched, not only physically, but in the sense of being emotionally moved. Moving through the chakras, or up the scale, there is a sense in which qualities of one become available to focus through the next. Even with the brief survey of the chakras which has so far been given, it can be seen that if the energies are working through from one chakra to another there will be, interacting in the heart: the potential warmth and grounding of the root; the flow and pure emotion, with creativity and sexuality from the sacral; and the fire, energy, sensitivity and aspects of vision and intuition from the solar plexus.

At first sight it may seem strange that the heart which is so often associated with feeling and emotion should be in the element of air. This element is usually seen as masculine, concerned with thought, and dry intellect. The heart tends to be associated with the feminine, with that which is tender, and with intuitive knowledge. How then do these interact with air?

The qualities of the heart itself include feeling, and vulnerability. The feeling or emotion however, is not the same as the emotion of the sacral centre. The quality which belongs to the heart is a second level of feeling. When touching, and being touched by the world, the heart opens and we can be at our most vulnerable. The emotions of the sacral centre are raw, the level of the 'gut reaction'. In the heart the feeling is that which carries attachment whether it be to people or to ideals, beliefs, or concepts. An important lesson to be learned with the aid of the heart centre, is *de*tachment without indifference. The element of air helps to link feeling to evaluation, and intuition to wisdom. The potentials in the heart are great, and it is the true centre of the inner wise being, but its opening and maturing can be a painful process.

It will have been noticed that the heart centre is the one which has had emphasis in some of the exercises already given in this book. This is because it is a wise centre, and one which acts as a bridge between the energies of the upper and lower chakras. Working from the level of the heart chakra gives optimum access to all the reserves of the being. It is the gateway to those centres whose activation helps to ensure reaching a level where discarnate meeting will be of value and quality.

The throat has blue as its colour, ether as its element and hearing as its sense. It is another gateway chakra in that it forms a group with the lower chakras, but is also a part of a trinity with the brow and the crown chakra. The element of ether does not relate in any direct way with the substance of ether as used in medical practice and early anaesthesia. As yet understanding of what it means in relationship to the throat chakra is limited. It is obviously the element of subtler areas of experience, and has con-nection to the so called etheric body.* It seems to be helpful for focus into more subtle levels of sound and colour. I consider the throat chakra, through my own experience to be the level at which inner psychological experience often moves into another dimension. It seems to be in its ineraction with the element of ether that this becomes possible. There is a high presence of potential in the chakra and its element for greater awareness of subtle planes.

The principle key word for the throat chakra is 'expression'. It is linked not only to hearing in the sense of listening, but also in the sense of how we make ourselves heard in the world. In its function as a gateway to subtle levels, and its link to hearing, it has an importance in enabling guidance to be heard. Clairaudience is connected to the throat chakra. That which we hear is often closely linked to that which we express.

The throat is the last of the 'developmental chakras' in the purely psychological sense. It has a double function in

* *See Glossary*

that it forms a whole, or trinity, with the brow chakra and the crown chakra. The crown chakra represents Soul; the brow Spirit, and the throat represents the joining of these to form incarnational intent, purpose and expression. In the throat chakra the voices of soul and spirit may be heard, and with the harnessed energy of the throat chakra these higher purposes may be voiced into incarnational expression. It is thus a very active and out-going chakra.

The next chakra on the journey upwards is the alter major chakra. In some ways this is out of specific alignment with the other chakras, and it has a reversed polarity. Usually the positive polarity of a chakra is in the front, or petals, and the negative polarity is in the stem. (Again these are not evaluatory terms, but more like the negative and positive poles in electricity.) In relationship to the physical body the alter major has petals in the centre of the face, and a stem at the back of the skull, at the top of where the neck joins the head. The positive polarity is in the stem. This stem has relationship to the old cortex of the brain, before the division of the brain into left and right hemispheres. It is sometimes called the lizard brain.

The alter major has brown ochre as its main colour, wet earth as its element, and smell as its sense. (The same sense as the root chakra). It is therefore also linked to instinctual awareness, but particularly to that point where this awareness touches into the racial consciousness. This chakra could be said to be the archetypal chakra, or the sensor for group, racial and collective awareness. Its action is largely pre-verbal, and primordial. It links into the primordial images and 'knowings' from which the myths have evolved.

It is a chakra of duality. The primordial images and knowings often have a negative autonomy, yet as they emerge into consciousness and form a mythology they also have deep healing power and embody spiritual truth and vision. When things are chaotic we live in a world of wordless nightmare. When the nightmare stills, arising from its darkness may come the very piece of insight and healing we need for the moment. So the alter major chakra is connected with the god Pan. In archetypal representation there is a duality about Pan. He is sometimes half man, half goat, with cloven hooves, forked tail and immense erect phallus, the god of rape, nightmare, panic and pandemonium. Sometimes the player of the Pan pipes, lord of the realm of elementals and devas, and the god of natural earth healing. This figure gives his name to 'panic' and 'pandemonium'. Such things run rife when we are out of tune with the myths of existence, and neglecting the substance of earth itself. When we seek to heal and be healed then the notes of the Pan pipes help us to find harmony in every way. The alter major is connected with finding this harmony.

The brow chakra has indigo as its colour, and radium as its element. It is beyond the realm of the purely physical senses, but links us to the spirit. Both the spirit of the times, and our own in-dwelling spirit. It is the centre of higher intuition and vision. As yet Gildas has said little about the element of radium in relationship to the brow chakra, but it seems to link to spiritual fire as a quality, and to be about change of substance and vibration which will help to lead us into the 'age of gold' of which he and other guides often speak.

It is not easy for us to distinguish indigo as a colour. It is as present in the rainbow as any of the other colours, but difficult to register and know and remember. It is a deep, deep blue with a touch of red, and is sometimes seen clearly in West Indian batik work where the colour is taken from the indigo plant. The 'wine darkness' of the Aegean sea is indigo. This colour is important to the development of our spiritual vision.

I shall come back to the brow chakra and its function in the raising of consciousness to the 'right' level for discarnate guidance. It is a place of interface between the psychological and spiritual worlds or planes of consciousness.

The crown chakra has violet as its main colour, but white and gold are also important to it. It is the link with soul consciousness and has been given the element of magnetum, by discarnate teachers. Information is certainly scarce about this element, but it seems to be connected with a force field, or energy field which applies on more subtle planes, and perhaps interacts with the physical plane, and our levels of consciousness. As collectively we gain more facility in awareness of other dimensions, and the groups of discarnates working from them, so the element of magnetum may be more fully conceptualized, and aid this contact.

Seen clairvoyantly the crown is the most magnificent of the chakras. Ideally it should always have its petals somewhat open, helping contact with the soul, and knowledge of the purposes of the soul for this incarnation. 'Going' to the crown chakra in meditation can lead to greater clarity about the purposes we have brought from the soul level into incarnation. It is through developed awareness of this chakra that we can feel fully 'in touch' with a sense of divine awareness. Yet the stream of consciousness and strength which flows in here, should always flow right through the central and subtle column, through the centre of each chakra, and down into the earth. The in-breath/out-breath, of inspiration and aspiration should be one which strengthens communicaton between heaven and earth, and vice versa.

There are simple breathing exercises which can be done to help this communication. These exercises also keep the central column clear, and enable energy to flow freely between the chakras in both directions.

The first is a pure breathing exercise, preferably performed standing up in an airy room, or outside. Become aware of your in-breath and out-breath, just as it is normally for you. Then start the in-breath just above the crown of your head, and bring the breath energy down through the centre of your body as you take it in. When it feels comfortable to do so, change to the out-breath, and continue breathing down through the centre of your body. Eventually breathe right out, through the root chakra, and into the earth. On the next in-breath, breathe in, as though from the earth, bring the breath energy up through your root chakra, and through the central column. Again change to the out-breath at the point where it feels most comfortable, and breathe out through the crown of your head. You can keep up this breath sequence for five to ten minutes, providing you are breathing relatively naturally without forcing and making yourself dizzy. Always start, and end with the out-breath downwards into the earth.

Visualization can be added to this basic exercise, so that it enhances consciousness of the four elements. (Earth, air, water and fire). If you can have access to a large tree, it is good to do this version with your back against the tree, and your bare feet on the earth. If no tree is available then you just need to make your visualization stronger. Once again it is best to do this exercise standing up. Visualize yourself as a strong tree. Feel the branches reaching into the element of air, and being warmed by the sun. Visualize strong roots going down into the element of earth, seeking the stream of living water in the earth. Then begin to breathe as before, first drawing through the branches of the tree the energy of air and sun (fire), and breathing that energy through the trunk of the tree, through its roots and into the earth, breathing out strongly into the element of earth and the stream of living water. Next breathe new energy up from the stream of living water, and from the element of earth. Bring this breath energy up through the roots of the trees, through its trunk, through its branches, and release it to the elements of air and sun. Again begin and end with the breath which breathes outwards into the earth.

On page 113 a map of the chakras is superimposed upon the egg diagram. In such an application it is not necessarily possible to draw all parallels to a full conclusion. Nevertheless the diagram may serve to help clarity as to which chakra is concerned with which area of development or being. It may also help to 'marry' the psychological approach with the esoteric spiritual approach.

The crown chakra links to the sun self, at least in Assagioli's original placing of that sun self. The brow chakra is in the middle of the higher unconscious, and the throat chakra at the interface between the higher and middle unconscious. The alter major chakra, in one sense should also occupy the area of the higher unconscious, but I would suggest that it should be seen as rather further out, at the edge of the three dimensional boundary of the egg, linking specifically with the collective unconscious. The heart is in the upper part of the middle unconscious. The solar plexus links almost directly into the field of usual consciousness, thus giving its connection with the ego centre of the personality, but also its link to the centre of the total being, for vision and fire. The sacral centre is on the interface of the middle unconscious with the lower

Diagram E

Relationship of the chakras to the areas of the psyche

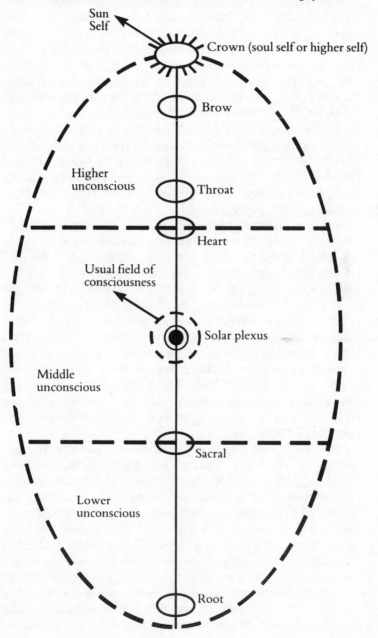

unconscious. This gives it connectedness to unprocessed material, but also to the creativity which is activated when that material begins to move nearer to the usual field of consciousness. The root chakra lies at another interface, that of the lower unconscious with the collective, but mostly in the lower unconscious. This shows its place in the process of incarnation and rooting, but also to early psychological material. This is often unprocessed material incorporating the experiences of the very young child, or even of the gestation and birth process.

In the diagram on page 47 there is a cross formed by the line of the emotional and physical journey of life going horizontally through the centre of the egg diagram, and the line of the spiritual and higher mental journey going vertically through it. A complementary chakra diagram could also be superimposed on the horizontal axis. This gives the chakras their relevance to the developmental stages of life, the root takes its place at the left of the diagram, at birth, and the crown on the right at physical death. The solar plexus remains in the middle, with its application both to the ego or personality self and the fully conscious Self with access to all parts of the psyche.

The present concern however, is with the vertical axis, and the activation of spiritual consciousness. I have given a brief outline of some of the functions and qualities of the chakras in order to show the way in which each energy is vital to the others. Together they form a team, but sometimes it is appropriate to use more energy from one level to another, or to gather as much team energy as possible to that level.

It is such realization which makes it possible to raise energy through the chakras, and to determine with full intellect the level at which, or from which, inner work is to proceed. The opening of the heart chakra gives the potential for a marriage of lower and upper chakra energies. At first it may mean that a certain emphasis falls upon the function of feeling as a means of evaluation. Gradually as spiritual training progresses it will become the centre where true wisdom, qualities of expression, warmth, creativity, intellect, higher mental awareness, spiritual vision, and all levels of the intuition are balanced and synthesized. Much work concerning inner guidance and discarnate guidance can be done with safety from the heart chakra as a starting place. This is why there have been consistent instructions in each exercise about 'breathing with the energy of the heart'. Working constantly from the heart chakra also has the virtue that it rarely brings an imbalance of emphasis in the chakra system, though the same is not necessarily true if the other chakras are overstressed as direct points of departure. There comes a stage however, in the serious search for discarnate guidance where it is not enough only to work directly from this centre of synthesis. A fuller and more precise approach to level, intent, and invocation is required.

CHAPTER 6

Procedure for Contacting Discarnate Guidance

I quote some 'standard' advice which Gildas gives to those who want to know better and more specifically how to be in touch with their discarnate guides.

'One of the most important key words in finding contact with your guide is that of 'dialogue'. So often you assume that we will come to you when you put out the message that you are ready, and that in that coming we will bring a complete knowledge of your thoughts, your wishes, your desires and your needs. You assume that we will bring the messages, and you will do the listening. This is not what we want. The expression of your joys, your sorrows, the way in which you see life is as important to us as it would be to any other friend. We need your questions to which we can respond. We too, learn from you and therefore value this aspect of dialogue

Furthermore we cannot, except in cases of great need or emergency, make all of the journey towards you. You have to learn to come to meet us. By the determination to find the meeting place, you signal your readiness for us to be a part of your lives, and also take some responsibility for the contact and its level and safety.

Using an awareness of the chakra system can both enable and focus this journey. The meeting place is at the level of the brow chakra. Here we contact your spirit and your higher vision, and are able to speak with it and through it. Here, if you train to make the journey correctly, you harness all the strength of your being, and can allow and open your awareness of other planes and areas of consciousness. Here you can weave together the fragments and nuances of experience until they become true subjective reality; an inner knowing of pertinent truths relevant to your being and phase of development.

To this meeting place we can come, reassured by your direction, invocation, intent and purpose. Here we can form with you a tender and precious contact, and participate in the building of a rainbow bridge between our different places and perspectives of life and growth. When you employ a certain discipline in learning to raise your energies through the chakras then gradually and certainly, guidance will manifest more fully in your life.'

There is a simple visual meditation which Gildas has given for reaching the place of contact at the brow centre. In the above statement he mentions 'discipline'. His interpretation of, and instruction about discipline is specific, but relaxed. Often on the spiritual path we can be hasty to rush into form or discipline, but there are attendant dangers. In the first flush of enthusiasm we may go to extremes of inner commitment. This may mean rising at an earlier hour each day in order to fit meditation or practise into an already busy timetable. It is far better, from the start, to see ourselves with honest sobriety in regard to these matters! Early rising and the promise of too much constancy too soon will shortly result in 'failure' to meet a self imposed standard. Failure, or back sliding on an enthusiastically made commitment brings disappointment in self, maybe even self blame and guilt. The whole project may get set aside with a sense of unworthiness, or unreadiness. Such a psychological climate is not conducive to spiritual growth.

Instead we are advised to endeavour to build in a sense of success. If in all honesty you know you are only likely to repeat a meditation or visual journey at monthly intervals, then let it be so. Yet let it also be a priority commitment, preferably entered in a diary as an engagement to be moved only for real emergency. Even in this case, as you think about the commitment you are making, know the frailty of human nature, and determine to make each occasion on which you honour this commitment, one of increment or success. If you give yourself prior permission to 'fail' from time to time, any hiccups in discipline will not have the same sort of negative psychological affect.

It is also human nature not to be satisfied with so liberal an interpretation of discipline! Bear in mind though that we are also told that it is to the degree to which honouring the journey to meet with our guides becomes a priority commitment that contact will become a meaningful part of life. As that contact becomes meaningful and joyful, so the incidence with which it is desired will tend to increase. Thus discipline builds itself into a meaningful pattern, and is not an empty ritual to which, after a while, only lip service is given.

There is a practice of meditation which aims to reach a certain level and stay there for a span of time. The preceding advice about discipline is pertinent to this. The visual journey to the brow chakra is relatively easy. It follows on from the practice of visualization which has been given in relationship to inner guidance and self discovery. *Staying* at the 'meeting place' or point of focus may be less easy. It can be helpful to make the approach with prior 'permission for failure'. Each time the attention wanders, and you find yourself planning your next day off, work schedule or shopping list, patiently return to the meeting place. This is part of the function of the structure of the given meditation. It provides a place to which to return for focus again and again, until the being is stilled and attention remains in that place. This is basically the essence and meaning of meditation.

The practise itself is a guided meditation which starts in the familiar meadow, representing the root chakra. A pathway then leads from the meadow up a mountainside. The goal is a plateau which lies *near* the top of the mountain, but not *at* the top. The upward path is a symbolic way of raising the energies through the chakras. The plateau represents the level of the brow chakra. On arrival at the plateau there is opportunity for exploration. The aim of this is to find a waiting place, or to form such a place with creative imagination. This place may be a 'travellers' rest', or a small sanctuary, or it may be an outdoor place warmed by the sun, with a clear view over the inner landscape. Somewhere on the plateau there is a spring, or source, of living water. Drinking from the source brings healing and refreshment. After this exploration you sit and wait with what Gildas terms 'open expectation'. (See below). You may bring to this place a seed thought, or a question, or even a mantram for asking your guide's name, which is quite simply, 'What is your name? . . What is your name? . . What is your name? innerly and rhythmically repeated. You may prefer just to sit and be still. It is to this waiting place that you return each time if your attention wanders. You do not need to do the whole meditation again, but just to focus back to the plateau. This focussing directly back, is an exercise in itself for moving quickly to a particular chakra energy level. In temporal time the waiting place at the plateau is about fifteen to twenty minutes. The whole meditation should not take longer than half an hour.

It is a good idea to build up a ritual which surrounds this meditation. Such as: always lighting a candle before you begin; sitting in front of a favourite picture; holding a crystal; wearing a special shawl or wrap kept for meditation. Rituals help the process of centring, and the building of an 'atmosphere'. If you are lucky enough to be able to set aside a special quiet room or meditation room in your home, so much the better, but a table, or a corner of a shelf, on which a few 'special' things are placed is quite adequate.

Here is Gildas' description of 'open expectation'.

'At the plateau, in the meditation for meeting with your guide, you sit with 'open expectation'. This means with a realization that guidance comes in many forms. If you have a structured expectation about meeting with a guide as a being, in a specific form, then this structure could blind you to experience. At the same time expectation is a positive energy which can make you receptive to guidance, or even to a meeting with your guide. It is a very delicate balance.

Know that guidance can come through a being who appears in form or in an 'energy body of pure light and colour. Know that it can come, even through a discarnate guide, as an inner knowing, without direct contact with a being. It can come as

specific words, either in your head, or with a definite
sense of hearing them spoken. It may come in mind
pictures, or symbols, or inner impressions, similar to
dream images.

The guidance you seek may not come to you while
you are actually at the plateau. Used regularly, this
meditation, as I have said before, will increase the
incidence of guidance in your life. After the focus of
the meditation you may dream a meaningful dream,
or pick up by 'coincidence' a meaningful book. There
may be a greater opening of 'creative thinking', a new
life contact may be made. Try to be aware of any
increase of synchronous events in your life, and to be
open to seeing these as the response of your guide to
your aspiration to contact.'

At the end of the waiting time at the plateau, you come
down the mountain, and return to the meadow. From the
meadow you sense your body again and your normal
surroundings, taking time for this re-orientation.

After such a meditation it is a good idea to close the
chakras, and protect them. A lot of misunderstanding is
currently around about the desirability of closing the
chakras. It is rightly felt that it is not good to be completely closed down, and insensitive to one's surroundings.
Sometimes 'closing the chakras' has been represented
rather like putting on a suit of armour, and by inference
condemning and shutting out the things of the world. I
feel that it is necessary to protect the chakras, though not
to armour them. They go into a different mode of
functioning for meditation than is really suitable for when
one is riding on buses, driving on busy motorways or
doing the other practical things in life. Protecting the
chakras is only a means of grounding yourself, and
reaffirming your own private psychic space. Surrounding
yourself with a cloak of light means that you affirm the
'light consciousness' of your meditation and take it with
you wherever you go, without being over sensitized and
vulnerable yourself.

Gildas offers a formula for protecting the chakras.
Remember that at the front of the body the chakras have
'petals', rather like the petals of a flower. It is these petals

which need attention after being in an open state for meditation. Only the seven main chakras need to be considered. (Without the alter major). The visualization is of each set of chakra petals closing in gently, but not tightly, so remaining flexible and sensitive, but holding the light within. The root petals, (pointing downwards, between the legs), and the crown petals always remain rather more open than the others. When all the petals have been relaxed in this way, an equal armed cross of white light* in a circle of white light is seen over the chakra, at the front, as a blessing. After this a cloak of light with a hood is drawn around you, and you make yourself specifically aware of the contact of your feet with the ground.

As with the earlier exercises, I give the whole meditation below, in such a form you can have it read by a friend as you do it, or put it on tape, to help you remember each stage. The closing down ritual is also included.

For this sort of meditation it is best to sit in an upright position with your spine straight. You can sit on the floor, with or without a back support, or on a chair, if you prefer. Be comfortable, but let your body posture be controlled and balanced. If you are able to sit in a lotus position, or with crossed legs, this is good, and makes the subtle energies of the body form a pyramid around you. It is not essential. (Those readers who have met me will know that my body shape does not easily accommodate such postures!) Although a lotus position or crossed legs are good meditative positions, it is *not* a good idea to cross the legs at the knees or ankles while sitting in a chair or on the floor. This makes crossed polarities in the subtle energy flow.

After your preparation ritual . . . close your eyes and be in touch with the rhythm of your breath, and feel each in-breath and each out-breath slowing down and becoming even . . . Let the rhythm of your breath help to take you into a meadow . . . Here activate your inner senses, so that you hear the sounds, smell the fragrances, see the objects and colours, know the textures, and taste the taste . . . From the meadow there is a pathway which leads up to a mountain . . . you are going to follow that pathway to a plateau, which is near the mountain top . . . climbing this

* *The cross is an ancient and pre-Christian symbol of wholeness and protection. A star of light can be substituted if preferred.*

pathway is symbolic of raising your sensitivity through the chakras to reach a particular level and quality of consciousness . . . Make the journey to the plateau in your own time, enjoying the pathway and the scenery along the way . . . When you arrive at the plateau, spend some time in exploring it . . . You will find, or can form with creative imagination, a waiting place . . . This may be a travellers' rest, or a small sanctuary, or an open air place, sheltered and warmed by the sun, but looking out over the landscape . . . There is also a source of living water on the plateau, from which you drink for refreshment and healing . . . When you have explored, go to your waiting place, and prepare to wait with open expectation . . . If your attention wanders, bring it gently but firmly back, each time to the waiting place . . . You may have with you a seed thought which you seek to expand, or a direct question related to guidance . . . you may rhythmically repeat a mantram relating to your guide's name . . . 'what is your name? – what is your name? – what is your name? The waiting time is about fifteen minutes . . . (Leave a gap on your tape) . . .

. . . It is now time to return . . . Drink once more from the source of living water if you wish, and take leave of any presence you may have met . . . return down the mountain, to the meadow where you began . . . take your time . . . then gradually become aware again of the rhythm of your breath . . . of your body in contact with your chair or the ground . . . open your eyes, and look around . . .

Before going about other tasks or concerns, with your feet on the ground, protect your chakras . . . this is done by visualizing the petals of each one gently relaxing in, like the petals of a flower, and holding light and energy within . . . Visualize an equal armed cross of white light in a circle of white light as a blessing over each one . . . Do this at the crown of your head . . . at your brow . . . at your throat . . . at your heart . . . at your solar plexus . . . at your sacral centre . . . and at your root . . . then affirming your awareness of the contact of your feet with the ground, draw around you a cloak of white light with a hood, so that you take light with you but are not over sensitive and vulnerable.

Once again the question or seed thought which you take into this meditation may at first be the one which came to you in response to 'What question should I be asking now?'

A visual meditation has been given here. It has been treated more as a meditation than a guided journey, and often body position will emphasise the subtle but important differences in these methods of approach. It is possible to lie down for meditation as well as for guided journeys, but in the stage where you are endeavouring to sense the differences in levels of consciousness it is 'psychologically' better and therefore more differentiating to have certain postures for each mode of interaction.

It is possible to raise the energies through the chakras without doing such a visual meditation, and some people may prefer this, as being again a method of differentiation, or because the visual approach is less easy for them.

In order to raise the energy directly through the chakras it is certainly best to adopt a sitting, or cross legged posture. You begin again by being in touch with the rhythm of the breath, and as that rhythm slows down and steadies, you sense the chakras, in alignment right through your body. The root at the bottom where the trunk joins the legs; the sacral about two fingers below the navel; the solar plexus in the diaphragm area, where the ribs curve and divide; the heart in the centre of the body, but on roughly the same level as the physical heart; the throat, at the front of the neck; the brow between, and slightly above the eyes; the crown, at the top of the head, its petals opening upwards. Remaining in touch with the breath rhythm is important here. You now begin to place your attention in each chakra in turn, starting at the root. Sense the chakra, remembering its colour note of red. Then using the breath rhythmically, and counting the in-breath-out-breath sequence as *one*, move upwards to the timing of six breath sequences to the sacral chakra. As you leave the root, place over it an equal armed cross or a star of white light in a circle of white light. Repeat the procedure with the sacral chakra, feeling into it, and being aware of its colour note of orange. When you move on to the solar plexus, do so to the six breath rhythm, leaving the protective symbol over the sacral chakra. The colour note for the solar plexus chakra is yellow. Go on up to the heart chakra, in the same way, moving into the colour note of green. Do not put the protective symbol over the heart chakra, but move on upwards with the same breath rhythm to the throat, and the blue note, and then to the brow and the inidigo colour level. Continue the meditation by remaining focussed in the brow centre, and feeling the flow of energy up from the heart. After the waiting time of fifteen to twenty minutes, move back down in a similar way, but put the light symbol over the crown chakra, letting its petals relax, and from that point following the 'closing down' procedure already given.

The reason for putting the light symbol over the opened lower chakras on the way up, in this meditation, is to prevent a loop back of energy, and also to modify the amount of energy which is being raised.

In my experience quite a lot of people who have used either version of this meditation regularly, have either met their guides clearly, or have felt an increased incidence of guidance in their lives. This latter is linked to the references quoted from Gildas, to the increase in synchronous happenings, a distinct inner knowing, the amplification of given knowledge in a creative way, and so on. (see Page 120.)

I want to pick up now, on the word 'dialogue'. This, Gildas calls a 'key word' in terms of access to guidance. It leads to the consideration of other practices for making and maintaining the contact with discarnate and inner guides. It is easy indeed to neglect our end of the dialogue in relationship to discarnate guides. Often there is a sense of awe about guides even as a concept. We tend to give them a lot of power, even before we know anything about them. If examples of wise discarnate guidance have been read, or heard, the qualities which the guides display, of foresight, insight, interpretation and compassion can make them seem God-like. We may expect them to be all knowing, and all seeing, and all wise.

People coming for guidance from Gildas quite often say to me: 'Why do I have to put questions to Gildas? Surely he knows what I am thinking, and can even tell me those things that I don't know that I *should* ask about.' This statement is not just an opting out of responsibility, it usually comes from a genuine puzzlement and confusion as to what can and cannot be expected from guidance. In order to form a relationship, it is often necessary to let go of preconceptions, and to separate guides from the God image.

This separation is sometimes necessary in order for people to feel *able* to approach guidance, and particularly for them to take the steps required to raise consciousness to the desired level. 'I am not worthy', can be a very great stumblingblock.

During my experience of counselling, and helping others to contact guidance, I have had the opportunity of working with cancer patients, using guided imagery, and a 'self discovery' approach to the disease, its personal meaning, and its healing. Often I have been amazed at the speed with which someone who was previously not even aware of the possibilities of either inner or discarnate guidance, will make intimate and clear contact with both. When there is intense need, a lot of the stumbling blocks and hesitancies are transcended. It is the need which creates the dialogue, and if communication is also seen as an energy, then it sets up a bridge to the meeting place.

I often tell groups who come to lectures, or guidance workshops, that it is essential, in the search for personal guidance not to regard my relationship to Gildas, and the way in which I communicate with him as a model. It is important not to set up an expectation of conformity which can limit creativity and vision in the personal guidance contact. Of all the people I know who are in clear contact with discarnate guidance, (and the number is swiftly increasing), there are many similarities, but no two experiences are ever exactly alike. Why should they be? All our relationships have differences, and each experience of guidance is very definitely a relationship.

So, the meditations to reach the right level of consciousness can help, but once the meeting comes about, how indeed does, or can the contact continue? Maybe we belong to that group of people who cannot mediate according to set forms. What then should be done?

There are many ways to start a dialogue, and alongside the concept of dialogue must go other advice which Gildas often gives which is 'Act as if . . .'. In other words, *assume* that your guide is there. Keep a journal and write it in such a way that it is, in part a communication to your guide. When you have time, even if it is only moments to reflect, or daydream, invite your guide to be present, or communicate what you are wondering about. Say it out loud, or in your heart, write down or draw it. Make it into verse or doggerel, and invite a response. Take a tape recorder and speak your thoughts and questions into it. Start a book entitled 'Letters to my Guide'. All these things signal your readiness, and are aids towards a sense of the reality of other dimensions into which your consciousness can unfold, or which will come at least part of the way to meet you.

At this point it may seem that the dialogue is rather one sided, more of a monologue in fact! The answer to this is to remember to be alert for the reply. There is more in 'being alert', than may immediately be apparent. It is partly summed up in what Gildas said about the 'increase in synchronous events'. It is the essence of what I mean when I say do not use what I experience as a model. Be open to *how* your answers come. As you invoke guidance you may become aware of certain phenomena, or signs. There could be a special quality or vibration of thought at certain times, a sense of a particular colour, as you get a new insight into something. Sometimes when Gildas wants my attention, and I haven't noticed, the left side of my nose will itch. Others have mentioned similar bodily 'symptoms' which appear when they need to listen or take note.

Maybe as well as a book entitled 'Letters to my Guide', you need to have a book entitled 'Letters from my Guide'. You may not get coherent messages, but in it you can list synchronicities, special colours, or key words. Remember that guidance can often come through symbols, or symbolic pictures. Dreams, with their rich world of symbolism can be representative of inner or discarnate guidance, and I will say a little more on this subject in the chapter on 'Symbolism as Guidance'.

With increased self observation, and a willingness to note things down the knowledge of the way in which you receive guidance will become clearer. The reality of the sense of being accompanied by a guide will supersede the 'as if' stage. There is rarely true scientific proof, but confidence grows as you validate your own inner realities.

It is always important to keep a sense of humour. The guides do! Usually their coming more clearly into our lives can have quite an impact. A friend whose guidance was getting clearer at a certain phase, but who was also used to living alone, found the sense of a presence with her almost all the time quite uncanny. She wrote a poem, which was humourous, but also had a touch of desperation in it. It included such lines as:

'When I'm out shopping, along he comes hopping.' and
'When I go to the loo I tell him to 'Shoo'!'

The second line quoted actually embodies a very necessary principle. Never be 'driven' or invaded by your guide. Learn to say clearly when their presence is inappropriate. They have things to learn about our way of life. A lot of the 'business' of modern living is quite fascinating to them, but remember that as they are on another time dimension they often have to learn to respect temporal time. If you feel 'driven' by guidance, ask first where this may be coming from in yourself, and next whether your guide is able to show the compassion and understanding, and give the freedom a true guide always gives. If anything about the experience of guidance is uncomfortable, always seek help, and confide in someone.

It may be of interest at this point to give anecdotes about how others relate to their guides, and the sort of 'signals' which reassure, and enliven the contact.

There is an example of contact with guidance which is sufficiently far from my own experience, or from the more 'direct' methods of communication to substantiate what I mean when asking others not to structure expectation, or to use my contact with Gildas as a 'model'.

A. is a friend who does not find meditation easy. She is not particularly at home with the language of symbols. Yet she lives with a great sense of trust in the reality of other worlds. Like many she often longed for this trust, and even excitement about the other worlds to become a more tangible and truly personal reality for her. At rather a low point in her life she was walking on one of the beaches of the island of Iona, when her attention was caught by a metallic object. When she picked it up, it had a sense of warmth, or specialness for her. It seemed to be some kind of lamp, maybe an ancient ship's lamp, with an inner cylindrical piece for holding a candle. *A.* kept the 'little lamp' as she quickly began to call it, near her, handling it, gently burnishing it, and feeling a sense of healing from a distinct energy around it, and in its very substance. The fact of finding it in such a spiritually meaningful place as Iona added to this sense of 'presence' which the lamp distinctly has.

Gradually a certain message associated with the lamp unfolded. A. had always been interested in architecture, stained glass, and the beauty of some of our churches and cathedrals. Now visits to these began to take on a distinct feeling of pilgrimaging. On every opportunity the candle of the lamp would be quietly lit, honouring the holiness and the aspiration of beautiful places of worship. Carrying a flame in this way, from one energy spot to another, linking the places together, forming a network of light has become a task of service in itself. No group is involved. It is often a lone pilgrimage. Yet the lamp has a special quality of appeal, and several of A.'s friends who might not otherwise be open to guidance, have enjoyed sharing quiet moments with the lamp's symbolic flame burning. The places of pilgrimage are by no means always large churches or cathedrals. Discovering delightful small ones in out of the way places seems to be something to which the lamp brings aid and inspiration. In a big cathedral town sometimes other smaller churches will be visited. In such towns, often the minor churches seem a little sad, or neglected with so much focus on the cathedral or larger place of worship.

Gradually it has become apparent that there is an accompanying discarnate energy with the lamp. There is a sense of a 'Benedictine' presence. A. does not 'see', but an added delight is the fragrance of incense. It is a particular and distinct perfume which rises quite separately from any incense which may have been used in a church, and is present when there is not other evidence of incense around. The 'guidance' of the lamp is linked solely to pilgrimaging. I find it a privilege to sometimes be able to go on such occasions. The guidance does not come in any specific communicative form. I have heard A. say that the 'little lamp is clamouring'. Sometimes this is just for 'an expedition', at other times she will have a distinct inner urging, or knowing, that it is time to go to a specific place.

The experience of the lamp has given a lot of joy, a reality of contact with other worlds, a specific task of service, and a healing reassurance.

It seems that sometimes we hit a sort of receptivity in ourselves, which enables us to be open to the way in which contact can come through. Suddenly we 'hear' it or 'see' it, or take the right actions to enable it to unfold. Afterwards we may be very aware of the 'hair's breadth' aspect of missing such as opportunity. Take the example of the lamp. On a beach it is so easy to pick up beach comber items, look at them and release them to the sea again. On this occasion *A.* might easily have done so, especially as she was feeling low. It was perhaps something in her need, calling out from her that enabled the synchronous events and the sensitivity of perception.

Another friend 'confessed' with some degree of diffidence about the mundane nature of her perception, that when she needs special reassurance, or help, or sense of her guide's presence, she looks for a sign. The sign she looks for is always a car number plate containing the letters GD. If she sees this she feels she can face anything, accept anything, and know that her guide is with her. She felt that the need for such a sign was childish, bordering on superstition, and in any case not to be borne out by anything either scientific, or 'guide like'. Yet on every occasion that she has been in need, the need has been answered by a sudden proliferation of GD's, even in a foreign country with unusual numberplates! Somewhat apologetically she asked for Gildas' comment on this, both as an attitude and as a phenomenon.

Gildas answered in this way:

'In such a circumstance you must be alive to the dangers of superstition, in that should this sign not work for you, it would be possible to expect the worst, and influence events by a certain negative attitude. Yet also you should not be ashamed of this simple trust in the ability of your guide to signal his/ her presence, and care. Often we are grateful for a 'prescription' which enables us to know how to reassure you or contact you. Though we ask that you should make every endeavour to meet us, we do also try to meet you, in so far as we are able to come into your material world. This signal comes from your inner guidance, your willingness to perceive, and ask, as well as from your discarnate guidance. When you are opening up to understanding of situations, and of life then so called synchronous, or acausal events do definitely increase. There is a magic which can be called into being which manifests in such ways. It depends to a great extent on your positive relationship to the universe, and your ability to perceive. Remember too, that we have a sense of humour. Such events, which satisfy you, are also pleasing in a 'light touch' way to us. Your material world is full of opportunities for our sense of 'play' and we only come near enough to this in some senses when you open the channel for our connectedness.'

So although we are enjoined to endeavour to raise our consciousness to help contact with discarnate guidance, they too are building bridges towards us, even to the extent of humourous participation in aspects of our 20th century physical environment! Some of the methods of opening to guidance which have been under discussion are somewhat removed from the more formal approach of raising the consciousness to the brow chakra level. Yet, my sense is that when the more straight forward approaches are employed, they are only effective when our need, our love, or our persistence enables a 'rainbow bridge' of raised consciousness to be built. Persistence, trust, responsibility, and integrity enable that bridge when the time is right.

CHAPTER 7

The Top of the Mountain: the Relationship of Discarnate Guidance and Inner Guidance to the Higher Self

The meditation for reaching the brow centre, or the plateau which is near the top of the mountain but not at the top, may also have opened questions about the top of the mountain, its symbolism and use in this scheme of exploration and training.

In making an equation between the chakra system and the mountain journey, the top must be seen as equivalent to the level of the crown chakra. The crown chakra is concerned with the essence of the soul, and of the bridge between the incarnate personality and that essence. It is the place where knowledge of the incoming Higher Will, and understanding of that can place many of life's apparently incongrous aspects into context. On the Egg Map it is the original place of the sun self. In spiritual terms it offers a level of linking with the aspect of the soul which is often called the Higher Self.

The teaching of discarnate guides almost always embraces the concept of many lifetimes, and of a span of evolution and experience which goes far beyond the confines of the present incarnation. Thus there are choices to be made about each incarnation; choices which relate to the nature of our psychological environment, our culture and place in that culture, our parents, our genetic inheritance, the degree of our consciousness of our spiritual task and our relationship to earth and the rest of humanity. All these choices are related to the sense of a Higher Will, a Soul, a Higher Self. They imply that there is another level of intelligence regulating our lives, and perhaps mediating for us in our sensing of that which is Divine. These aspects are not sub-personalities, because they are not strictly part of the pure psychological level of personality. They are certainly recognised in a more transpersonal approach to psychology, and may have some interaction with sub-personalities. They will certainly have interaction with that place within, which we may define as our Inner Source, or Inner Wise Being, yet they are not specifically that Source or that Being. Neither are they discarnate guides, if those guides are seen as distinct entities having an independent experience beyond the total complexity of that which we understand psychologically, spiritually, or transpersonally to constitute our experimental being. The Higher Will, Self and Soul are integral parts of our discrete totality, though having a distinct voice, and purpose. At times in our lives when we are concerned with the important development of the little ego we may feel ourselves to be in almost diametric opposition to these higher, supposedly wise and governing aspects.

The personality self may rail against the so called choices with which it seems burdened. I know that many times I have told my Higher Self or Soul, that it has 'bitten off more than my personality can chew'! This latter complaint holds an existential truth, yet it is through just such a complaint that a greater truth eventually dawns. We don't have to do it all in our own strength. If our souls, or Higher Selves representing the soul, chose it then we can draw on their strength for understanding, support and direction. Furthermore if those choices were made on the basis of previous or other experience of incarnation, we can draw on that collective strength, from beyond the finite limitations of that which constitutes the direct physical experience of incarnation. All this strength and reassurance pours in through an open and activated crown centre. Making a link from the crown chakra (higher Will), to the solar plexus (lower will), can bring a sense of that strength in moments of need. It is done quite simply by visualising the golden light of the higher Will coming in from just above the crown of the head, through the central column, and into the solar plexus chakra. Feel the solar plexus flooded with this light and strength, and then breathe the light of the higher Will out through the petals of the solar plexus.

The visual journey up the mountain leads on beyond the

plateau, with its link to the brow chakra, to the temple at the top of the mountain which is representative of the crown chakra. In some respects one might say of this mountain meditation that when you are ready to go to the top of the mountain, and curious enough about it you will go. It can thus be used as a personal voyage of discovery to see what is there. In one respect it is a journey back to the spiritual source, to connect with the impulse and plan of being and incarnation. It is good to use the given imagery in this creative way, and I hope that in giving a set meditation for reaching the top, and for suggesting the sort of connections which may be made there, the opportunity for creative exploration is not cut off.

To any stage in these meditations, or to any aspect of the exploration of inner guidance, you can continue to take the question from the initial 'question exercise'. (See page 65). In this meditation, going to the temple at the top of the mountain, or the source, there are other questions, or thoughts, or explorations which can relate to a deeper understanding of your connectedness with your soul or higher self.

An enquiry which people often make when they come to Gildas for guidance is 'What is my task or purpose in this life-time?'. The feeling which lies behind such a question is one with which many of us are familiar. If we could but get a sense of what we are meant to be doing, then it would be relatively simple to go out and do it! As one may suspect, things are not that simple. The task or purpose of our life may be about finding out, for ourselves the answer to that question, and about exploring the nature of being. Western society has been very much focussed on goal orientated thinking in terms of life function. What we do in terms of a career has all too often become what we *are* in terms of identity. The question so often put to the young in their formative years reflects this, 'And what do you want to be when you grow up?' As though 'being' only starts at a certain point, and when you can put a label on it.

One of the more positive aspects of the present economy with its high levels of 'unemployment' could be that the living of life is less goal orientated, and the search for identity less tied up with labels. The danger is that the polarity from goal orientation too easily becomes passivity and indifference. It is helpful to be able to identify, at least, a way of being, or an incoming information of purpose. This may not, and often should not, lead to a sense of having to prove that purpose, but more to a way of expression in whatever we happen to be doing, wherever we happen to be in the journey of life. Life choices can be clarified by such identification. Yet when choices may not apparently be available, it also helps in changing the situation from within. There are various reasons why the 'status quo' may have to remain, but sensing an inner key word relating to mode or purpose can still be greatly releasing and enabling. The artist, perhaps trapped in but dedicated to looking after an elderly parent, can either feel frustrated, or may determine to do the whole job more artistically. Thus changing the environment, using the giftedness for arrangement, the eye for colour, the whole aesthetic way in which the job is done can help to change the nature of the task in hand and make it more roundedly fulfilling. Once identified, the inner purpose, giftedness, or mode does not have to die, or suffer all the pain of frustration, it can be helped to some means of expression whatever the situation may be.

In a conventional teaching post I suffered frustration because I had identified strong key words relating to my own mode of being, as 'transmutation', and 'healing'. I could focus on these inwardly, but also needed to feel them more in outward use. It did not seem possible at that time to change my life completely in the outer sense. It was only when I began to lay more emphasis on my interaction with parents about their problems with their children that I felt that this mode of being was finding expression. In this way my general frustration with teaching lifted for a while. As I expressed more of that essential aspect of myself, I also gained confidence in it, and so eventually could make big life changes for myself. Yet knowing that aspect of my being more fully, in a certain sense it no longer mattered, whatever the situation I knew an important essence of my expression, and could make space for it.

Knowing this mode of being, has connection with the higher Will, or sense of soul purpose. It is not necessarily a task to be totally manifested in terms of outer identity, but can be greatly releasing to the inner expression. The knowledge of this basic core of identity may have become confused by the expectations of society, teachers, parents, and parent figures. Going to the source, or the temple at the top of the mountain can result in finding a valuable clarity or key word.

There are other things which may become clearer at the source, or the temple at the top of the mountain which represents the crown chakra. Esoteric teachers and guides, either discarnate or incarnate, including Gildas, give us to understand that incarnating souls choose their parents. The higher self, having an overview of the life about to be undertaken, and the opportunities for evolution which can be presented, makes this choice with a number of factors under consideration. These will include genetic inherit-ance, (the type of body we shall have), racial, historical and cultural inheritance, and the general psychological environment. In other words, all the positive and negative factors which will enable growth. If the life is one in which there is a quest for spiritual awareness, then understanding these factors more as choices can be very helpful. It increases the dialogue between the higher Will and the lower will. These factors may remain unconscious or pre-conscious but their affect involves each human in incar-nation.

Discarnate guidance may come strongly into the picture at the crown centre too. The higher Self, the input of the soul is not, by definition, discarnate guidance. Yet at this point, at the source, those who see, help, and support our evolution, and perhaps group evolution, are likely to be present, in essence, even if not in defined being or visibi-lity. The crown chakra is an interface area indeed, and the deep wisdom, knowing and recognition which is the characteristic of true guidance from wherever it may come, can interact powerfully for us if the consciousness is successfully raised.

In many ways the journey is similar to that which was taken to the brow centre, or the plateau near to the top of the mountain. Because it is an all encompassing journey, potentially leading to the source where personality inter-acts with soul, and soul with the divine, the visualisation is more complex. An attempt is made to include fully all the different factors in this raising of the consciousness. Unless you are working with a specific teacher, or in a supervised group, it is best to take this journey as a visual one, and not to attempt to do a continuation of the direct raising of the energy through the chakras, which was given as an alternative for reaching the level of the brow chakra. The imagery and symbolism carries an inbuilt facility for the psyche to precede at its own pace, according to its own wisdom. The more direct method may be too straight and demanding when taken to this level.

The power animal has a place in this meditation, and leads to the concept of 'the gate-keeper'. When you go near to a threshold, it is advisable to have a gate-keeper. In this scheme of things this function is fulfilled by a combination of the power animal, and the inner wise being. As stated before, the power animal symbolises the instinctual wisdom, and it is good to have that working for you. The inner wise being harnesses the basic wisdom of your psyche, with all its qualities of intuition and discrimination. If you invoke this aspect, then you can make a true and safe connection between the inner and discarnate levels, or the inner and soul levels, if the timing is right for you. If you are accompanied by instinctual power and inner wisdom, and the timing is not right for you, you will not be tempted to force the pace, nor be disappointed in yourself, or your discarnate guide, or your higher self, or soul, if you do not make the connections. You will know that you are where it is wise for you to be, at this particular point in your life, and be able to accept that calmly as an enhancing piece of guidance and inner truth.

Before you begin the meditation, consider the sort of things you may like to have greater clarity about, in light of this preceding discussion. Maybe you seek insight into your essential 'mode of being'. Maybe you want to know more about the nature and purpose of some of your choices concerning this incarnation. Perhaps, on the first occasion, you are focussing more exclusively on a raising of consciousness, or going to the top of the mountain 'because it is there'. Your only particular area of purpose may be to seek contact with your discarnate guide. All these things relate to the 'intent' of the meditation for you.

Try to be clear about your intent without over structuring it. From your intent, the invocation which you are making to these levels of being follows almost automatically.

I will not describe the meditation further, but give it now in the form of direct instructions. It can be transferred on to tape if you wish. Although this is a very visual meditation, and brings in aspects of earlier guided journeys, it is treated here as a meditation. Therefore it is better, at least at first to take an upright meditative position as described before. (See page 121).

Close your eyes, and let your body be poised, supported if necessary, and relaxed . . . Be in touch with the rhythm of your breath . . . each in-breath and each out-breath, and feel this rhythm in your heart chakra gently activating your heart energy . . . Flowing with the breath rhythm, go into your inner space, and find yourself in a meadow . . . here, take the opportunity to activate all your inner senses . . . see the colours and the objects . . . hear the sounds . . . smell the fragrances . . . know the textures . . . and taste the taste . . . You are about to embark on a meditative journey to a temple at the top of a mountain . . . it is the same mountain to which you go when you wish to visit the plateau which is near the top, but not at the top . . . From the meadow you can see the mountain, and the pathway which you are going to take, and you know that climbing this pathway is symbolic of raising the energy through your chakras . . . be aware of your reasons, or intent in making this journey . . . Now call on your power animal to be present with you, and ask it to accompany you to the plateau level to which you have been before . . . see whether there is any other talisman present with you, or a special one which you wish to take on this particular journey . . . then, accompanied by your power animal, take the pathway which goes up the mountain . . . you can see the plateau to which you have been before, but the top of the mountain may be rather misty, perhaps with a faint colour tinge to the mist . . . look about you as you go, take in the landscape of your journey, knowing that once you have been this way you may wish to return . . . about half way up the mountain you will be joined by your inner wise being, either in full visible form, or by a sense of the essence of the presence of that being . . . Continue then, to the plateau with your power animal and your inner wise being as companions . . . When you get to the plateau, spend some time renewing your acquaintance with

*this waiting place, and your sanctuary or travellers' rest here . . .
drink from the source of living water . . . You are going to ask
your power animal to remain on the plateau as a guardian or
gate-keeper, resting but watching, and waiting for you . . . your
inner wise being will continue the journey to the temple at the top
of the mountain with you, and your discarnate guide may come to
meet you at this point whether you have already met each other or
not . . . Again there may be a definite presence, or just a sense of
the essence of a being and companion whose quality, fragrance
and texture is reassuring to you . . . You can now see the
pathway which leads from the plateau to the top of the mountain . . . you may be going upwards into a lightly coloured mist,
but the pathway at your feet is clear . . . after a while you will
become aware that the pathway turns into steps, beautifully and
purposely carved, and that you are coming to an outer courtyard
to a temple of light and colour . . . in this outer courtyard, or
perhaps series of courtyards, there may be some ritual which you
know needs to be performed before you enter the temple . . .
perhaps you need to change your robe, or your shoes . . . to walk
through a pool in this outer temple court . . . Whatever it is,
there is a part of you which knows, and your wise being is with
you to affirm, help and support . . . When you are ready, the
temple doorway lies ahead and is open for you . . . spend the
next ten minutes of this meditation in your crown chakra temple,
exploring it, or being there in silence, with your consciousness of
your quest or intent in coming to this place . . . (leave a ten
minute gap on your tape) . . .*

*. . . Before you leave the temple, there may be a blessing for
you to receive, or a gift to be given to you, or presences to take
leave from, but it is time now to do these things, as a preparation
to leaving and taking the return journey down the mountain . . .
(3 minutes . . .) . . . It is time to leave now, but you do so
knowing the way here, so that you may return at any time you
wish to do so . . . come out of the temple, back into the outer
courtyards . . . you may need to go through a ritual again, or to
reclaim your own clothing if you put on a special robe for entering
the temple . . . your wise being, and perhaps your discarnate
guide are with you to help and support . . . from the outer
courtyard go down the steps, and then down the pathway which
leads to the plateau where your power animal is waiting, and will
greet you . . . drink again from the source of living water if you
wish . . . take leave of your discarnate guide at this point if a*

meeting has taken place, and continue the journey down the mountain with your power animal and your inner wise being . . . both may return to the meadow with you, or your inner wise being may take leave of you at some point on the path . . . when you come to the meadow, spend a few moments again feeling your feet in contact with the earth of the meadow, and the familiar scenery here . . . finally take leave of your power animal, and become aware of your breath in your heart centre, your body, its contact with the chair or ground . . . let your feet make contact with the ground of your outer environment . . . open your eyes . . . move and stretch . . . and come peacefully and gradually back into your everyday world . . . then centring your body once more, protect the chakras, thus holding light and energy within, and available, but making yourself in a less open and vulnerable state, suitable to the demands of everyday life . . . Visualize the petals of each chakra relaxing gently inwards like the petals of a flower, and put an equal armed cross of white light, or a star of white light in a circle of white light over each one . . . Do this at the crown of your head . . . at your brow . . . at your throat . . . at your heart . . . at your solar plexus . . . at your sacral centre . . . and at the root . . . draw a cloak of light with a hood right around you and affirm the contact of your feet with the ground.

This meditation may need to be repeated from time to time to reap all the benefits and insights from it which have been suggested, but by using it there can be an increasing sense of access to all layers of the being. There can come also a gradual sense of that experiential learning which enables knowledge of different planes of consciousness and reality in a way which no given 'map' of consciousness, or intellectual discussion or even poetic description can give.

If previous exercises in this book have been followed over a period of time, and with the built in meaning of the symbolism in this meditation, it is unlikely that you will encounter undesirable incarnates. If ever you are in any doubt in these exercises or meditations, return to the starting point, (usually the familiar meadow), and through the closing down routines to your normal everyday environment.

Protection is something which I have tried to make implicit in the design of these explorations, and some of the discussions around them. I have spoken a little more explicitly about it in relationship to the 'closing' of the chakras. Your own observation, resolution, and firmness are always the best defences. It is possible to over stress the need for protection. The exploration of inner and discarnate guidance is basically something which brings expansion, joy, and a fuller sense of life itself. It is not necessary then to approach it fearfully or defensively. I have however included a reference in the bibliography for further reading on this subject.

CHAPTER 8

Symbols and Dreams and their Relationship to Guidance

The world of symbols is a very interesting one which has a distinct life of its own. When first exploring the inner worlds, and their symbolism it is all too easy to lay too much emphasis on interpretation. 'What does it all mean?' is a natural response, but too fine a definition at too early a stage can bring certain limitation. Symbols almost always have more than one layer of meaning. They speak to the past, the present, and the future at one and the same time. They also speak simultaneously from different parts of our beings. Waiting for each level of significance to unfold can give insight into these different parts. A slick interpretation of something will tend to mean that it is put aside, as 'done', neatly stacked in the 'out' tray of our inner filing system. Symbols often need to be left in the 'pending' tray for quite a long time. It is only in this way that their capacity to work for us can begin to be understood.

The living quality of inner symbols is found in their ability to change, even when, apparently they have been given no attention. If some of the exercises in this book are repeated at intervals, sometimes new symbols will emerge each time, though often the old symbol will be there, but somehow changed. More of it, or less of it; a different colour; more friendly, or less friendly; transformed, but yet showing its relationship to its previous form.

In the work with the inner landscape I made a suggestion that things might be noted which needed attention. If there is a bog in your inner world, you may note that it needs draining in order to form more fertile land. Having noted this as a symbolic insight, outer life probably takes over. However good your intentions you do not return to this inner task for a while. When you do, you may find to your amazement that where there was bog, there is a field of corn. The clue may be in your outer world. It seemed to take over, but perhaps you were being more creative there, clearing away things that needed to be cleared, and so your inner world reflects that activity. Often if you look back to the time when you got energy and impulse to do that clearing in the outer world, it will correspond with the time you made that inner recognition. The reverse can happen. Having seen what needs to be done in the inner world, you may neglect that, and be feeling also more and more overcome by events in the outer world, really 'bogged down'. A visit to your inner space will probably confirm that, the bog is bigger, or deeper or blacker than you recommend.

If you work at the inner level but not at the outer, it is also amazing how often the changing of the inner symbolism will ease the outer situation, and enable what seemed previously stuck and impossible to change.

The symbols can also be exacting and confronting in their commentary. You may think that you've been clearing everything up in the outer world, but when you return to your inner landscape there is no field of corn, only the bigger, deeper, blacker bog. In the clearing you thought you were doing, you may not have been true to your inner self, and the symbols will reflect this for you. If you learn to listen well to them, they can save you from breakdown or illness. Few manage this, the function of disease is full of symbolism in itself.

In these examples I have used reference to symbols in a certain way. There is a level of interpretation implied. A relatively straightforward example has been used, but I have tried to illustrate the way in which symbols live for us, and with us, giving valuable information when we learn to listen and observe in the right way. *Having* a symbol already marks activity, progress, or dialogue between the inner and outer worlds, or different aspects of our beings. Therefore treasure it, mull it over, take it out and look at it from time to time, honour it as a gift, and gradually it will speak its language to you, and you will be able to communicate with it. It is not that symbols should remain uninterpreted, but there are stages in that interpretation. The mental or intellectual analysis should be the last, not the first approach, if it is guidance which you are seeking.

In the book 'Man and His Symbols',* C. G. Jung makes an important distinction between signs and symbols. There are many signs around us, attached to familiar objects, such as the Red Cross, signalling First Aid from a well known organisation. I quote:

'Man uses the spoken or written word to express the meaning of what he wants to convey. His language is full of symbols, but he also often employs signs or images that are not strictly descriptive. Some are mere abbreviations or strings of initials, such as UN, UNICEF, or UNESCO; others are familiar trade marks, the names of patent medicines, badges, or insignia. Although these are meaningless in themselves, they have acquired a recognizable meaning through common usage or deliberate intent. Such things are not symbols. They are signs, and they do no more than denote the objects to which they are attached.

What we call a symbol is a term, a name, or even a picture that may be familiar in daily life, yet that possesses specific connotations in addition to its conventional or obvious meaning. It implies something vague, unknown, or hidden from us . . .

Thus a word or an image is symbolic when it implies something more than its obvious and immediate meaning. It has a wider 'unconscious' aspect that is never precisely defined nor fully explained. Nor can we hope to define or explain it. As the mind explores the symbol, it is led to ideas that lie beyond the grasp of reason . . .

Because there are innumerable things beyond the range of human understanding, we constantly use symbolic terms to represent concepts that we cannot define or fully comprehend.'

Jung is speaking here of a universal and conscious need to use symbols to aid interpersonal communication, about those things which we know to have a deeper meaning which as yet can only be expressed symbolically. Although concepts and conceptual language are constantly evolving, they remain, by definition, limited. The symbol is unlimited, and if we let it, will aid the evolution of concept.

* *See bibliography.*

In inner work, symbols may be used with a certain consciousness, but they also begin to arise from less conscious levels of our being. They become a powerful and pertinent means of intrapersonal communication. When our unconscious parts wish to reveal information to us, in terms of our own, immediate, universe of the psyche, that information is preconceptual. It cannot, therefore, flow in words. The unconscious aspects speak in any case more through the right brain than the left, and therefore have less access to the language of words. Specific words do not come until a concept is more fully developed. Symbolism then is the collective and personal language for that which is pre-conceptual, or has meaning beyond the limitations of concept. It is thus a language which is beautiful, exciting, and awe-inspiring. With its aid, that which is undifferentiated, dark, or shadowy, may be differentiated and born into the light of awareness. Like any birth, the more sensitively it is attended, the more satisfying and full is the experience.

Words are not entirely inappropriate to or unknown by, these more unconscious facets of ourselves. Sub-personalities, power animals, inner wise beings, and others may be quite verbal and specific in their communication. Yet often the form of their appearance speaks much more about them, and their relationship to us. Our culture is very verbal. Language is more and more deeply imprinted into our total constitution. Yet in listening to the language of inner levels, care should be taken to recognise its symbolic content, the clever pun or play on words, the 'double entendre'. I shall speak more of this aspect in commenting on dreams.

In the exercises in this book a conscious, and guided level of symbolism is used in order to invoke individual inner experience. It has already been discussed how this 'imposed' symbolism may be seen to have a certain objectivity, whilst each inner experience of it will be subjective. In using symbols to help in your self understanding, and in order to interpret the inner guidance of the psyche, it is this subjective aspect which needs to be considered. What does it mean for *you* that your tree of life is a 'willow' or an 'oak'? Does the form of your symbol have any particular personal resonance, significance, or memory, in relation to your life attached to it? Why has your psyche chosen this tree, rather than another to represent for you 'the tree of life'?

If you look too soon at a dictionary or encylopaedia of symbols you could read such information as:

'*Willow:* an enchanted tree, sacred to the Moon Goddess. The weeping willow depicts mourning, un-happy love and is funerary . . . The withy is an emblem of childbirth . . . Strength in weakness; contrasted with the pine or oak which resists the storm and is broken by it, the willow bends, gives way, springs back and survives.'

'*Oak:* Strength; protection; durability; courage; truth; man; the human body. The oak is often associated with thunder gods and thunder; sky and fertility gods have the oak as an emblem, hence it can also represent lightning and fire.'*

Such comments are interesting, even helpful, but they could overshadow the personal memory of: 'There were oak trees all down the road where I once lived as a child. That was a time of my life when I really felt alive', or 'When my marriage was new, and full of vitality and promise, there were willow trees by the river where we walked on our honeymoon. I often gain joy from that memory'.

This latter way of relating to a symbol is the stage which Jung calls 'association'. Evoking all the personal response to the symbol which has presented itself, and considering the added messages and information which that response brings.

The former example, explanations, and scholarship from a book, encyclopaedia, or dictionary Jung calls 'amplification'. This sets the symbol in a wider context, and may bring additional insight, but is never more important than the personal level. When you let a symbol be 'alongside you' when there is no immediate association, days, weeks or even months later, you may suddenly remember, 'of course, *that's* what my psyche told me by giving that image'.

It may sometimes be frustrating not to know, to have to wait, only to feel a vague, or perhaps awe-inspiring

* *Quoted from* An Illustrated Encyclopaedia of Traditional Symbols *by J. C. Cooper. See bibliography.*

awareness for what has emerged, but the unconscious is very specific in its symbolism, and it is worth being patient, and yet receptive to this rich language.

For many people symbols just do not 'come'. A common comment is 'I feel as though I'm making it all up, creating it, making it happen. It all comes from a mental and rather active level'. This may be so, but it is not reason for disillusionment. Out of all the myriad symbols which can be chosen, at a specific and given time, your psyche working through the mental level selects certain symbols, in juxtaposition to each other. They often yield just as interesting, revealing and valid material in association and amplification as those that 'just appear'. Giving attention and respect to the symbols which you get however you feel you arrived at them, will encourage the intrapersonal communication, and allow it to evolve.

There is usually some difference between symbols which come as a result of guided imagery or meditation, and those which arise from dreams. Dream symbolism emerges from the deeper recesses of the unconscious, and is often more encoded, further away from rational or logical sequence. We find ourselves in bizarre situations, following seemingly unconnected events, inappropriately dressed, or performing skills we know little of in everyday reality. Full consideration of dreams is not the scope of this book. There is a wealth of good material available about them.* Yet they are pertinent to a discussion of symbolism and also to inner and discarnate guidance.

It has been scientifically established that we all dream, probably every night, whether we actually remember the dream material or not. Further it is accepted that dreaming sleep is essential to mental and physical health and well being. Yet comparatively few people pay attention to their dreams, or consider that the seemingly illogical events of them may hold valuable information. I have already suggested that *having* a symbol is a significant stage in intrapersonal communication which should not be underestimated. The fact of scientific establishment that loss of dream sleep affects mental and physical health reiterates this strongly in relationship to dreams. The symbolic life

* *See Glossary*

does not even have to be remembered at the conscious level, but it has an important integrative work to do within the recesses of the psyche.

If you are reading this book you are probably in the process of commitment to self understanding. If you already remember your dreams it makes sense to begin to record them, and watch the sequences, and the range of symbolic language which comes to you from them. The mere recording of dreams, and occasionally looking through them, will often result in insights about them, and a gradual movement towards fuller understanding of your personal symbols. Recording in a loose leaf notebook can help in later being able to sort out specific dream themes. These themes may be seen to relate to certain cycles in your life, to times when the same concerns are coming up in conscious life for consideration.

In my own dream life I have a series of dreams which have a 'moon theme'. They usually occur around the time of the full moon, and come from my feminine side, which was very wounded. I know that just noting and attending to these dreams, without always analysing them helps in the healing process of that aspect of myself. I also know that when I have those dreams, I may need to check out with myself the space or lack of space being given to the feminine. Sometimes these dreams are like wonderful gifts, beautifully affirming a process to which I have given a lot of attention over a considerable time span.

Another recurring dream theme for me is one which I call 'the Victorian dreams'. They alert my attention to my freedom of choice, sometimes in quite a humorous way. I have a tendency to revert to patterns of choice which do not really belong, or fit with my personal values, and visions about my life now. Receiving a Victorian dream, puts me on warning about this tendency. On the other hand a Victorian dream may remind me of aspects of the old structure which I do want to take forward and so help me to look for balance.

The Talmud speaks beautifully of dreams as 'letters from our souls'. Obviously they will differ in impact and intensity. Some dreams have about them such a power, that they remain with us for a lifetime. We remember them, return to them, and are affected by them. Other dreams may too often be dismissed as being caused by 'the cheese at supper time'. By all means be aware of the different levels and qualities of dreams, but remember what I have said about 'having' a symbol, and do not reject any of these communications out of hand, whether they be 'cheese dreams' or only small remembered 'snippets' from what you know to have been a longer dream whose greater substance has not remained in your awareness.

Obviously then, dreams can be considered as important communication in the area which has been termed 'inner guidance'. I know from personal experience that they can also reflect the process of relationship and communication with discarnate guidance*. In this respect they do also represent the close cooperation and interdependence between inner and discarnate guidance. If you sense the closeness of your discarnate guide, but have difficulty in communicating, or receiving answers to your questions, it can be particularly valuable, revealing, and helpful to clearing the contact to give more attention to your dreams. Because dreams come from deeper recesses of consciousness, and are encoded they get through a certain barrier in our awareness which Freud termed 'the censor'. The symbolism of dreams can help us in a gentle, or obscure way to come to accept things we may otherwise be defensive about. It is these same defences which may sometimes make it difficult to 'hear' our discarnate guides, and it is my view that they will then often use the vehicle and language of dreams to support their communication to us.

Dreams can be 'incubated'. If you seek deeper communication on a certain theme, you can 'ask' your psyche for a dream, and it will often respond. In the same way, as part of the communication with discarnate guides, I feel that they can be asked to 'send' you a dream. This can be part of the 'as if' communication (before you have direct experience of your guide, see page 125), as it can be of the more conscious communication with such a guide.

It may be noticed that once you start to work with guided journeys and meditations, the pattern of dream life changes. You may dream more dreams about the themes

* *See 'Seven Inner Journeys'. Ruth White and Mary Swainson. published by The C. W. Daniel Company.*

on which you are working, thus amplifying the information coming from the more conscious work. You may remember less dreams, perhaps indicating that there is enough material to deal with coming from the other level of input.

To those who have difficulty in remembering dreams, I would say that guided imagery work may help here, or certainly compensate for the non-remembering. It is also true that in the scientific experiments about dreaming, where the subject was woken up whilst in dreaming sleep, there was always immediate memory of the dream. I have known people who are determined to capture their dreams to set an alarm clock to wake them at varying periods during the night. With a notebook and pencil to hand, this is often successful. It is important to have the means of noting a dream easily available, and to try to put down at least some key words on waking. Sometimes a dream is so vivid in those waking moments, that its possible to convince oneself that it will not be easily be forgotten. By the time you're in the bathroom, it may well have receded without trace. What is certain is that as soon as you give attention to the inner language of your being, there will be a response, and the communication will tend to increase.

It is worth noting that people who have difficulty in remembering dreams can often capture hypnogogic and hypnopompic images more easily. These are the names given respectively to clear images which sometimes come at the edge of sleeping, or at the edge of waking. Noting these down will often act as the trigger of 'attention', and result in greater dream remembering facility.

The guide-lines for the interpretation of dreams are the same as those for working with symbols. Note them, live alongside them, make drawings of them. Associate to each symbol and each phase of the dream. 'Listen' to the statements which the dream is making. Just telling a dream to a friend, with a sense of reverence for it, can begin to help its language to unfold. When you feel you have all the associations you can make, then it is the time to ask others to help you to amplify them. Sometimes friends will have good insights, but you should always feel free to assess whether those insights speak to you or not. Beware of friends or dream interpretation books giving such categoric messages as 'a knife in a dream means a broken marriage'. Such statements are not based on personal association, and are to some extent symbolic in themselves. A knife *could* mean that some tie is being cut, depending on other circumstances of the dream, but that which is happening may not relate to outer events, or may mean the cutting of something which has been very binding to you, and hampering in your process.

Some people give too much power to the symbol, or to the dream, in a fatalistic sense. Symbols and dreams are messages, and commentaries, offering guidance. They are neither portenders of doom nor foretellers of good fortune. They may warn of the need to change, some of them may look quite clearly into the future for you, but of themselves they have no power to influence events. Only the individual can do that, and with right attention to dream and symbolic information positive power over one's life can increase.

Nightmares are the dark side of the dream, where material is coming from more hidden, shadow levels of the unconscious. They can be very frightening, but often, if the symbols are faced, and brought fully into consciousness, they will transform in very special ways, releasing a lot of energy to the dreamer. It may not be possible to effect this transformation alone, but there are counsellors and dream groups, where help is available.

A very interesting aspect of dreams and the language of symbols, is the statements which they lead us to make about them in linguistic terms. Dreams may seem irrational and mixed; symbols may seem incomprehensible, but listen to the way in which you find yourself describing them. Dreams in particular, often have clever turns of language, which are part of the dream information.

Thus at a time when I was about to make an important decision, a dream warned me that I was not in possession of all the relevant information. It took me back to a time in my life when we had owned a dog called Pinocchio. This was also a time of indecision, and living out the consequences of some choices, which with hindsight might have been different. We often shortened the dog's name to 'Nocchi'. This shortened name was used in the dream, and in recording it I spelt it as above. It was not until I read the dream out in a dream group, that someone picked up on that name, the pronunciation of it, in its shortened form was always 'No-key'!

In describing a moon dream, I stated that I was walking along a 'causeway in the sea'. The symbolism of this dream was very potent in itself, but looking at the word 'causeway' led me to many insights about the way which I had 'caused' and the way which it might be possible to 'cause' as an alternative.

Another dream about my whole relationship to life took me to the sand dunes near Liverpool. I have specific associations with these, but the dream held even more significance when I fully considered the word 'Liverpool'. There was a reference to health in that too, which prompted me to revise my rather 'liverish' diet.

Numbers in dreams can be very pertinent too, and lead one to know that the psyche does not give any dream information by chance. It may take some decoding, but precision is its forte.

I hope I have said enough to show how relevant dreams are to guidance, and perhaps to inspire further reading and investigation of this perennially fascinating area of the psyche.

In the next chapter of this book, Gildas comments on questions which are often put to him about guidance. One of them deals with the difficulties of communication between their plane of existence and ours'. The technical difficulties are enough, but it follows through that if information is being given which goes beyond the individual or present journey of concept, the only way to open that limitation may be through the language of symbols and images. The symbolic world then is part of the structure of that rainbow bridge of communication, not only from one aspect of our psyche to another, but from one dimension of being to another.

Before leaving this section about symbols, I want to honour the promise to comment on some more aspects within the possibilities which have been presented by the conscious level of symbolic structure in the exercises. By gathering such comment here rather than interspersing it in immediate juxtaposition to each exploration, my aim has been to leave time for your own natural association and assimilation of symbolic material. Having now tried to explain more of how symbols work, I present these comments not as interpretation, but as amplification.

The inner landscape itself is highly symbolic yet it has its own reality which is demonstrative of the intrinsic essence of the symbol. In health the inner worlds are interdependent with the physical world which is generally accepted as real. Exercises which lead into experience of the inner worlds rely on archetypal symbolism for their structure. In the introductory paragraphs to this chapter it has been demonstrated how the archetypal, and to some extent objective imagery leads into subjective experience. Many of the structural symbols speak for themselves, but groups have sometimes found it helpful to have them divided up in so far as this is possible, into their relationship to the masculine and feminine principles. Before doing this it is necessary to arrive at some definition and description of these principles themselves. When speaking of a principle it is important to remember that it does not speak of the conditioned image of 'man' or 'woman' but of complementary aspects which form a whole, and without which, in equal balance, there is no full access to wholeness.

Interesting things happen when groups attempt to make lists of the qualities of the masculine and feminine principles. Either there is a reversion to man/woman conditioning, or qualities get mixed up with functions. Thus I would define creativity, and power, for instance, as functions. This means that they can be approached either from the masculine or the feminine principle, depending on the quality which is being brought to them. They are most effectively functional when the masculine and feminine principle are in balance within them, or when handling them. I have come to know that any list of the qualities of these principles is controversial, but here are my suggestions:

In the feminine principle: negative; receptive; yielding; gestating; passive; containing; fecund; nurturing; hollow; soft; opaque; defending; sheltering; nurturing; calm; rounded; diffuse; dark; undifferentiated; indirect; lunar.

In the masculine principle: positive; thrusting; active; providing; fertile; phallic; building; hard; initiating; moving; pointed; aggressive; focussed; transparent; light; differentiated; direct; solar.

The inner landscape journey, (see chapter 2), had the four elements as its first basic structure. Generally the elements of earth and water are considered to be feminine, and those of air and fire, masculine.

Within each element the symbols which it was suggested may be found would classify into masculine and feminine as follows:

In earth: The forest, the fertile plain, the marsh or bog, the cave, the pleasant path and the pit are mainly feminine.

The mountain, the desert, the rocky path and the island are mainly masculine.

The tree of life is unclassifiable into either masculine or feminine in this way. It is best seen as a symbol of balance, in touch with each of the elements. (See page 42).

In water: The river of life; the sea and/or lake; the waters of peace; the whirlpool and the underground stream are mainly feminine.

The source or spring; the rapids and the icy place are mainly masculine.

In air: The area of low pressure; the place where it is easy to breathe, and the resting place with cooling breeze are mainly feminine.

The whirlwind; the place where the sun always shines and the mountain top are mainly masculine.

In fire: The living fire (in so far as it is contained and warming fire); and the hot springs are mostly feminine.

The volcano and the lighthouse are mainly masculine.

N.B. It is definitely more difficult to catagorize the masculine and the feminine in the fire element.

In considering all these symbols and how they appear for you in your inner worlds, it is not just masculine and feminine balance which needs to be noted, but general balance. Is any element comparatively more sparse than another? Is the pit too deep, or the living fire out of control? What is the state of the tree of life? Is it strong and well rooted, or more fragile? Once the lack of balance is noted it gives the insight as to where work may be done to rectify it.

A similar approach is needed with all the structural symbols. In the meadow for instance, there may be too much or too little growth; it may be too large and uncontained, or rather small and cramped, with very high hedges. The mountain may be more like a small hill than a mountain, or perhaps too steep, and therefore difficult to climb. In the world of symbols, if you work at things they will modify. If they change too quickly or immediately, to your command, you may not be allowing yourself to see how the status quo is at any given time.

I am not necessarily suggesting that all things have to be modified to a norm. See how they feel to you. It may feel good to have access to a raging fire, or to an exceedingly lush and fertile meadow. These things may help to reveal your strengths to you, or areas where not enough energy is actually channelled into the outer world. Consideration of all these factors, in a rather commonsense, but full and free ranging way will help guidance to unfold.

Lastly in this chapter I should like to comment on the relative significance of different power animals.

Obviously it is not possible to go through the whole range of animals, which may have been met as power animals. For extended knowledge I do suggest in this instance, that you refer to an encyclopaedia of symbols such as the excellent one already quoted in this chapter. (See page 145) Always bear in mind your own associations, and your right to accept or reject amplifying information.

For the general role of animals in symbolism, I quote first from that same encyclopaedia:

'Instinctual life; fertility and teeming life; the instinctual and emotional urges which must be transcended before man can enter into spiritual realms; passive participation; animal nature in man. . . 'Under the semblance of animals the Egyptians worship the universal power which the gods have revealed in the various forms of living nature'. Friendship with animals and ability to communicate with them symbolizes the restoration of, and re-entry into the paradisal state, the Golden Age. Animals accompanying or helping man on quests depict the different aspects of his own nature, or the instinctive and intuitive forces of nature as distinct from the intellect, will and reason.'

Shamanic belief around the power animal is concerned with the empowerment of the individual for life, health, and healing. When you are 'on terms' with your power animal, you function well from all levels, and protected by its strengths and instinct. Your power animal will not only speak to you, but will 'dance' for you, and with you, in the 'dance of life'. Rhythms, and rhythmical chants are used to help a sense of the animals reality and presence.

In the exercise where there was the first meeting with the power animal, (see page 73), I stated categorically that although your power animal might in the natural state be very wild and fierce, it would, in this setting be your friend and protector. This is partly because when the true power animal is invoked it *is* so, and partly because it is my belief that in this time we can be on friendly terms with the animal kingdoms. There may be a great deal to rectify in our misuse of them in the outer world, but a lot of the symbolic battling with the wild animals which is the substance of ancient myths has been done. In the current spiritual and personal explorations, especially of the Western world, there is a re-engagement with the myth, but at a new level. Therefore it is important to recognize that which has been achieved for the collective, and as a part of the collective dream and is safely recorded in the ancient myths. If this recognition is made, then there is no need to continually retread old ground. Claiming and expecting the friendship of the power animal, in the inner world, is one of the ways of making this affirmation, and of validating old traditions. It is also a way of moving forward from a point which is appropriate to now.

Usually the more naturally wild the animal which comes to you when you call, the more primitive is the instinctual level from which it comes. The tamer animals could be said to be nearer to human consciousness. Like the talisman, you may get additional or different power animals according to the sort of journey you are making, and what your psyche has 'on offer' to you. Do not be dismayed if your power animals seems to be something relatively calm and retiring like a rabbit, a mouse, or a hare. All these animals have strong instinctual qualities, and when you amplify your own association to them by reference, you can respect what they mean for you.

The next and final chapter is Gildas' own, where he comments on questions which he is frequently asked about guidance.

CHAPTER 9

Comments from Gildas on Questions frequently asked about Guidance

One of the most basic group of questions which Gildas is often asked is:

'Does everyone have a guide? Is it likely that we have more than one guide? Are all guides for women male guides, and guides for men female guides?

Gildas:

Everyone has a guide and at the right time, direct contact may be made with that guide. There is a great sense of 'family connectedness' on those planes which are less accessible to your personality selves. The soul structure, going into the group soul is a very complex one, and within this there is guidance and concern for each incarnate being.

If discarnate guidance is not conscious, or direct, it will manifest from the level of the higher self, or the soul. Guides and helpers in communication with that level of the being, and helping to act as a bridge to the earth plane will endeavour to help the personality self to fulfil the chosen purposes of the soul self for a given incarnation. In some phases of life it may seem that guidance comes more from knocks on the head and kicks from behind, than from the sort of potential for loving dialogue which has been suggested in this book.

The value of giving attention to guidance lies partly in the increasing likelihood of achieving conscious communication. Such contact is part of the paradigm of the Aquarian Age.* But it also lies in gaining more sense of equanimity, insight and consciousness with acceptance, about life patterns and life experience. It establishes a sense of communication with purpose, and with an interconnectedness at subtle levels, which means that life flows, more smoothly though still within its ups and downs. Such consciousness allows synchronous events to happen, and to be noticed, and decreases the incidence of the knocks on the head and the kicks from behind.

We cannot say often enough that we want and need the contact with you too. Yet it must be forged on a level of mutual dignity, trust, love and respect. In some ways it might be said that guides are 'god-parents', with vested interest in the connection of soul to personality. As the connection becomes more alive, so the 'god-parents', can take on more of an equality relationship, and we can all become co-workers in consciousness to achieve better conditions for planet earth and humanity in incarnation upon it.

It follows then, that there is often more than one guide. Some guides are poised for the timing of direct communication, others are more like helpers, members of the soul group, endeavouring to give a sense of nearness and support. These helpers may never become completely differentiated for you. It is those of us who have a specific communicative task, in relationship to incarnation and planet earth, at this time who will seek differentiation, and to forge the tender contact.

It is necessary to explain that on this plane of life we are more diffuse in our being than you are on earth. Our boundaries overlap more. In order to make out contact with you more personal, and more tender, we assume fuller personality than is natural to us in our own environment. As part of a response to another question I will explain more about the confusions which can arise about the identity of guidance, but staying within the direct relevance of the present question, it can be true to say that more than one guide may be in direct communicative contact. This contact may come from different areas of the group soul, or there may be contact with a personal guide, and also with a group soul teacher. It is all

* See Glossary

rather more complex than may be supposed from your perspective, but as I go through the questions here I will try to build up a fuller picture for you. I would point out here though, that the person, who over coffee at one of your conferences on esoteric subjects, was heard to claim contact with forty two guides, probably had more of a problem on her hands than an advantage!

Your guides may be either masculine or feminine, and many women have female guides, while many men communicate with male guidance. Often there may be a sense of both aspects manifesting, but as I hope to demonstrate later, these will not necessarily be different guides.

It is always necessary to watch for confusions in expectation which may carry through from the inter-face into psychological understanding. To suppose that men always get female guides, and women males, could arise from a confusion with the Jungian psychological premise of the 'anima',* and the 'animus'*. Because of possibilities arising from our dif-fuseness of being there may often be a tendency for a woman to relate to the masculine principle of guid-ance and a man to the feminine. This could some-times be a result of anima/animus projection, and such possibility needs to be kept in consciousness, because it is one of the 'hiccups' in guidance which can lead to 'colouring' in the communication. The need for attention to psychological level transparency arises again and again.'

The next set of questions which I have suggested that Gildas should comment on in the context of this book, run in this way:

'Who is my guide likely to be? Is it someone I have met in another life? What is the nature of my relationship to my guide, and of his/hers to me? Can you, Gildas, tell me who my guide is, and give me the name?'

Gildas:

'Your guide is usually a member of your group soul. This means that there is a common task and interest

* *See Glossary*

in certain patterns of evolution, and experience of incarnation. This means too that those who are incarnate, help our task of guidance from another plane, in the degree to which you enable us to help you.

It is quite usual then, for your guide to be someone you have met in a previous life time, though not necessarily so. Not all members of a group soul will meet each other during the course of incarnations.

It is within the scope of this question that there comes the matter of our more diffuse sense of being on these planes. In order to communicate with you, we 'clothe' ourselves in a personality. This personality is usually near to one which we have lived in during an incarnation, particularly an incarnation where we may have learned and been able to hold a wise way of living, in tune, and harmony with the universe, and specifically with the spiritual dimension.

For instance, in personality terms, Ruth experiences me partly in the 'dress' of my last incarnate personality which was as a Benedictine monk, in France, in the fourteenth century. This was a very necessary 'clothing' for the earlier days, of our contact. (In terms of Ruth's present life.) The disadvantage of too specific a personality as far as we are concerned is that it becomes a limitation. 'Gildas' was a popular name in France at the time of that last incarnation, and there is historical documentation of more than one monk called 'Gildas'. All too often this is seized upon as 'proof' of my existence, and identity. If I were to accept this identification it would mean that I was too much seen in that ancient context. The personality which was a monk in fourteenth century France is incorporated into the being who now manifests in guidance as Gildas, but 'I' am not limited by that personality. The more total, and diffuse being with which I am reunited on this side of life includes so much more than one aspect of incarnate experience.

Thus there are many potentials for the 'clothing' of personality in which I might have chosen to manifest to Ruth. Part of the governing factor for this present choice has been where Ruth feels able to link most positively with me. With her sense of connectedness to France, then that incarnation of mine proved to be a good bridging point in this respect. It is actually much more satisfactory now, for me as a being, that Ruth is able to relate to my 'energy body', and my essence, without needing the monkish clothing or personality so specifically.

I explain this at length because it has a lot of bearing on the question as to whether you all have more than one guide, and also on my ability or otherwise to tell you who your guides are, and give you their names.

As previously explained it is possible to be in contact with more than one 'guidance entity'. Yet often if you consult different sensitives, mediums, 'psychics', or psychic artists, it will seem that at each consultation a new guide is seen. A lot of confusion and distrust arises from such experience. If it can be seen then that your guide is a composite being, seeking the 'clothing' for manifestation to you which is capable of making a strong resonance with you, perhaps the confusion can lessen. Thus one sensitive person may see your guide as an Egyptian woman, another as a Red Indian warrior, another as an inscrutable Chinese being, and yet another as a Greek healer. These are not necessarily a plethora of guides, but different aspects of the same being, resonating more to the consciousness of the different sensitives, perhaps, than to your own specific rapport.

It can also happen that your guide may choose to take on different 'clothing' when helping you in different ways. So taking the above example as a possibility, the guidance entity represented may manifest as an Egyptian woman in order to inspire creativity; as a Red Indian warrior to teach the laws of spiritual connectedness with nature; the inscrutable Chinese in order to speak philosophically, and the Greek healer to help develop healing ability. Any or all of these may manifest, either in turn over a given period, or else at different phases of the life of the incarnate person concerned.

Add to all this our diffuseness, and sensing of each other in our 'energy bodies', and in essence, rather than in personality form, and you may perhaps begin to see why it is no easy task to introduce a guide, and give that guide a name. Such introduction can even be a hindrance rather than a help in establishing guidance contact. If you are given information, it sets up an expectation, and you tend to channel your energy towards that expectation. It is possible that in giving a name to your guide, and a 'clothing', I may hit on a possibility for his/her manifestation which is not necessarily the easiest one at the precise place in time where you are, for the building of that bridge of communication. Focussed as you then might be on the given form, it could mean that the condition of 'open expectation'* necessary to guidance contact was less possible for you to attain.

Add to this the tendency which most people have eventually to discount experience which comes as the result of over formulated mental suggestion, and you have another stumbling block. If there is too much information, it leads to distrust of experience. When you meet the presence of your guide without pre-formed expectation, or specific information, there is much more potential remaining for assimilating and validating your own experiential way.'

At this point is seems necessary to include a specific question about the group soul concept to which Gildas refers so many times:

Can you tell us more about the group soul? Can you explain something of the mechanism of reincarnation? What about twin souls? Can you comment on hierarchy?

Gildas:

'I can, perhaps give best understanding of the group soul, and the parts of the soul which come into incarnation, thus making what you call the 'mechanism' of reincarnation by giving you some images.

* *See page 119*

First of all imagine a tree, with its roots and its trunk, its branches, its leaves, its fruits and its flowers. This may be said to be an image of the group soul. The main trunk of the tree represents the group soul being. The main branches represent different aspects of the consciousness of that being. They emerge from the main trunk, and are in communication with it. The minor branches represent individual soul consciousness, and the leaves, fruits or flowers represent personalities which have been or will go into incarnation. Thus each time there is an incarnation, it is not exactly the same being which incarnates. It is a different aspect for each incarnation. After incarnation, and before it the separate aspects are in communication with the minor branch which is the soul. As incarnate experience is built up, so each flower, fruit or leaf, contributes that experience to the consciousness of the minor branch. In turn the minor branches contribute the differing ranges of gathered experience to the main branches, and the main branches contribute it to the trunk of the tree, or the group soul being. The 'higher self', is the gathered consciousness of any one of the minor branches, or soul stems, the processor for the soul, of all experience. This can be experience which is gained between incarnations, when gathering experience on this side of life, as well as when an actual personality is in incarnation. Any particular tree, or group soul may have a specific range of interest in the field of building up awareness, and this will constitute the total consciousness of the forest of trees. There are many forests of trees, and many trees in each forest. Guidance will usually come from some part of the tree, from a main branch, or from a minor branch which has built, or is functioning from a particular angle of evolution.

Continuing the image of the tree, twin souls would be seen as two minor branches joined at the point where they also join to a major stem, so sharing the consciousness at a basic level, and more closely than other minor branches. Each soul has a twin soul, so the minor branches come out from the major branches in pairs. As well as twin souls there are aspects of the same soul, after the minor branch has split off into its own particular consciousness. These aspects are the flowers, leaves or fruits of the tree which pass into incarnation. Up to seven aspects may be in incarnation at any given time, usually not meeting, but seeking complementary experience to speed up the process of consciousness. Each individual soul stem, putting out leaves, fruits or flowers into incarnation will usually select a variety of incarnations in both genders, in the search for, and expression of, balance.

In totality, and in the way in which it is too often related to at the human incarnate level I dislike the concept of hierarchy, and the traps which it can hold. A hierarchy can only really exist in terms of linear time. It is a linear concept. Thus within your experience of linear time, at any given moment, or existentially, a hierarchy exists. At that time there will be a relating to beings who seem 'more advanced', or 'less advanced', according to which area of potential they are linking into in the existence of that moment in time. Beyond linear time, the form is more like a wheel, or a sphere, where all is co-existent, and past, present and future do not operate in the same way. With the spherical or circular form there can perhaps be a glimpse of the way in which it is possible to link into any or all levels of being, without having to experience them hierarchically.

To return to the image of the tree, when all aspects of the tree are in conscious flow the one with the other, there is total resonance and flow of experience, and this resonance co-exists with the more limited and contained consciousness of each of the separate parts.'

Another pair of questions which are repeatedly asked are:
What is the relationship of the guides to Divinity? When you speak so much about soul choice, the higher self and the higher Will, does that mean that you do not subscribe to the concept of free will?'

Gildas:

'As guides we are part of humanity. In accordance with what I have said about the concept of hierarchy away from the linear time, we are part of the body of human consciousness seeking union with the Divine, or on the journey of return to the Source. As we manifest at this given time, we are seeking to communicate from a different perspective, and by that communication to help to raise awareness. Yet I see all aspects of humanity, from whichever plane we may be functioning as part of the concept of Divinity too. I would not conceive of Divinity as a separate being, but more as a composite state of being, and therefore also in a process of growth, expansion or becoming. Divinity is not a finished, or a static state.

Within this sense of growth, or becomingness we might be seen as functioning from the part of the system which enables every hair on every head to be counted and known, every sigh heard, and every sparrow which falls noted. Through unconditional love, and co-creatorship Divinity may be known as a wholeness, and inclusion, within which there is no need for separation. It is in working towards the communication of that, and holding it as a trust, that we, no more and no less than all may do so, manifest our relationship to Divinity.

Here is my understanding and perspective in relationship to free will. There are certain choices made by the soul, or higher self as to desirable experience which needs to be differentiated. Personality aspects are sent into incarnation for this purpose of differentiation. During the process mistakes are made, and other personalities may carry into incarnation a need to redeem, those mistakes, this is what is meant, in general terms by 'karma'.* The incarnate personality *has* free choice, but to the degree to which that free choice can be aligned with the choices of the higher self, or the higher will, so life will tend to flow more smoothly, and take on greater meaning, purpose, and fulfilment. The difficulty often lies in the concept that anything 'Higher' is likely to be judgemental, and the giver of hard tasks, frowning on joy, pleasure and self evaluation in accomplishment. This is not so at all. The aim of the higher self is redemption and transformation of karma rather than over focus on retribution. Redemption and transformation bring joy into life, and unite spirit with matter. When the personality self insists on retaining free will, it insists on a certain tunnel vision. However within the definition of free will, that is a valid choice, and is always available!

The theme which I have asked Gildas to comment on in the next section concerns difficulties which arise in the interpretation of guidance. There is no doubt that it does often need to be interpreted, particulary in the sense that all responsibility should not be handed over to the communicating entity. Even very specific guidance is only another perspective, and we are free to act on it or not. Familiarity with a communicating guide always helps. Over the years I have come to trust Gildas with joy, but part of that trust is built on knowing him as intimately as any friend I have. His guidance is not perfect. The communication systems are not yet perfected. The trust comes from a key quality which I experience from Gildas, and that is integrity. I have asked him then to comment on the following questions:

'It sometimes seems that guidance 'works' for some people but not for others. I am not speaking here of the mechanism of receiving guidance, but of what happens in people's lives as a result of guidance. I have known examples where guidance is fluent and specific, but somehow eventually, promises which have been made fail to 'match up' in terms of our physical environment. You have often spoken of difficulties which arise from your perspective in the matter of communication. Could you speak more of these difficulties, and perhaps also comment on the area of discrepancy in response to guidance? I sense that these things are somehow linked.

Gildas:

'This is in many ways a key area in the establishment of trustworthy links between your plane and ours. What has to be remembered is that the territory

* *karma - see Glossary*

is still relatively uncharted, especially the territory which is opened up by the movement into the Aquarian Age. The very words of 'mediumship' and 'channelling' have unfortunate associations with particular atmospheres of communication from these planes. Although it is understandable there has been too much emphasis on 'evidence' in communication in an objective sense which is almost impossible to establish. This emphasis leads away from the individual capacity to evaluate subjective experience and truth. It leads to the handing over of responsibility, to the totally abandoned trust of 'the Innocent', and to the 'testing out' and acceptance of material in rather a naive way. Much of the substance of this book is dedicated to coming to guidance from a level of personal strength and self knowledge which will not only minimize these difficulties, but will make it increasingly possible for there to be more and more 'conscious' or 'mental' mediumship. You, Ruth, have had a lot of often painful resistance about becoming an 'empty' channel, and being seen by others mainly as 'the medium for Gildas'. This resistance is right. The pain has often come from a lack of vision and perspective in others. I like to think that together we are working towards changing the image of both mediumship and guidance. The limitations have to be stated and seen, just as they do in any other form of communication. Guidance has to be separated from clairvoyance, and from the mysterious power which some people assign to us of being able to influence and change the future for them. My function is as a teacher, supporter, helper, companion and friend, not as a fortune teller or decision maker.

Too often we discarnate guides are seen as being able to give precise information about things which are rooted in your physical reality, and time dimension. Thus we are asked to say where and precisely when, houses are for sale, or money will be available, or even to manifest the money! I have even been asked to supply the name and exact address of someone's twin soul. In putting out these sort of expectations there is a lot of confusion about the way in which it is possible for our different dimensions to interact. When answers on this level are received there is a lot of confusion as to the energies which are coming into play in the channelling.

At this stage I know that you can probably quote for me numerous instances where guidance of this kind has been remarkably accurate. There are certain things with regard to future potentials and possibilities which we *can* see very clearly. We cannot however, put them concretely and precisely into your time dimension. One of the most difficult things in our communications to you is the bridging of the time dimension. I will speak more of this, but in the present aspect under consideration where there is concrete precision of guidance, a number of factors may be at work. Firstly there may be confusion in the 'medium', of use of psychic energy, and the receiving of spiritual guidance. Many mediums or channels are very psychic in their own right, independent of their guidance. It is this energy which can often lead to precise vision as to time, place, manifestation of resources and so on. The true psychic energy is much more kinesthetic, and linked to your immediate incarnate energy field than is the spiritual. When there is not a clear distinction about these two energies, the guidance will be very mixed. The discarnate communicator will be affected by the psychic awareness of the channel. The vision which is coming from that level is bound to affect the teaching which the communicator gives, because it affects the proportion of the future which is seen, and the dimension on which it is seen. The thing to recognise is that such psychic clairvoyance is not the energy with which the spiritual communicator *can* be concerned.

Yet when the communicator gives substantiation to what is then seen clearly by both medium and guide as a potential for the future, these issues get very confused. The spiritual level of guidance is being 'coloured' by psychic perception, without this being conscious. The trouble is that psychic perception is by no means constant or consistent, and the more the level of the medium is raised to that of the spiritual communicator the less does that degree of psychic kinesthetic perception work. Without awareness of this, highly 'coloured' dialogue may continue between the medium and the guide, with the precise information which has come to be expected in rather physical terms becoming ever more unreliable. Because such a situation arises from a basic lack of training and awareness of the energy levels in the medium it is very difficult for the discarnate communicator to find the vocabularly with which to clarify what is happening. The expectation is at the same time too simple and naive, and too structured, strong and limiting. Often the only way out of this situation eventually is for a discarnate communicator of integrity to stop communicating, and to hope that the self exploration for the medium, which comes from that cessation will lead to the sort of insight which makes a resumption of a new level of communication possible.

In another sense, however, spiritual guidance may be accredited with success in relationship to very material matters, and time, when other factors are in operation. To explain this I must try to describe how we do see the perspectives for which you are able to speak about. We see energy and light patterns not only around you in the auric sense, but in relationship to your life, your life choices, and the plan of your evolution. We do not see your time dimension clearly at all, and part of what we have to learn in being communicators, is that something which we may see as 'soon' could be immediate for you, or could be ten years ahead! However we do have a very strong perception of *timing*. Because of the energy factors which we see, we can know if synchronicity is going to be particularly powerful for you or not. We can also see geographic factors, and relate them to these energy patterns, so that we can suggest areas of living which may better help you to strike the true 'chord' of your life. We can often identify the key words which relate to the basic functions which it is most profitable for you to explore during your lifetime, or at a particular stage of that life. We can see your

auras, and your chakras, and thus identify the energies which are working strongly within you, and
those which may be blocked at a given moment.

Gathering all this information together may make
it possible for us to say things about material or
monetary possibilities, or to advise that more or less
energy be put into a cherished project. Thus if we see
that the timing is right, and that the synchronous
energies are with you, and say so, it perhaps inspires
you to act, to be more consciously attuned with
synchronicity, and so to achieve the right sequence of
events in relationship to physical things like houses,
investments or practical projects. When this happens
you tend to ascribe to us this power of fortune telling
or of being able to influence events. We cannot make
synchronicity happen, we can only see its potential.
We can only know that when you are centred and
focussed into something you yourselves attract positive progressional energies, therefore if we see a right
timing we can support you into it, or suggest that
you wait, in order to avoid frustration. The choices
are yours', you are basically the authors of your lives.
You have to learn to take risks. We can sometimes
help those risks to be more calculated ones, but the
future is set in motion by your input. It is not laid out
like a map which we can read for you, at least in those
very specific physical terms.

Our main difficulties in communication lie in the
form which that communication should take. In
conscious or mental mediumship we mainly use the
vocabulary of the medium, sensitive or channel.
Unless specific vocabularies are known by the channel information tends to be very generalised, needing
perhaps too much interpretation to be of accurate use.
An example here is related to communication which I
have been asked to make over a period of time to
some radionic practitioners. It was not necessary for
Ruth to do any deep study of radionics, but before
the communication could be developmental and in-
formative enough it was necessary for her to learn
some of the specialised vocabulary, so that the words
I seek to communicate with are stored in her 'mem-

ory bank.' This is also partly why it is necessary for those who seek guidance to give some background information, and formulate questions precisely. This procedure usually gives the vocabularly which can enable my replies to be as personal as possible.

On this dimension we communicate with each other less in words than through direct thought transmission. Thus when you seek contact with us, and by such seeking give permission for that contact we may speak to you through your thought patterns. As far as you are concerned of course, this is a less identifiable pattern of guidance, and is not an immediate dialogue in the way that response in words can be. Putting our thought, though into your available vocabularly and conceptualisation is a difficult technical process for us. Part of my taking on of the 'dress' of a monk is because in that existence, I was very interested in words, thus I help myself to make verbal communication with your dimension by contacting the incarnate experience of that interest and facility.

Sometimes we are trying to communicate concepts for which you have no framework, not just in the individual range of the medium, but in your society or world. Such communication is extremely difficult. Trying to explain the timeless dimension presents particular obstacles since your language and concepts are so linked to time, and to a linear understanding of time. In endeavouring to form a framework for new concepts, it is often only possible to use images or symbols. Yet if you learn to give greater value to the power of the symbol to open up ground for the expansion of concepts, this can become a very rich field for interaction.

We love the opportunity to communicate with you. The 'clothing' of ourselves to come nearer to you, enables us also to come nearer to the dimension of incarnation, and this can be a 'playful' pleasure and delight to us. We respect the serious nature of your questions, and aspirations of course, and understand that often you are weighted down by incarnational concerns. We are no longer weighted by these in the same way, so your world holds fascinations for us. We long for communication to be so easily identified and formed that there can be more opportunity for sheer enjoyment, humour and fun together. We can help you to be both more rooted into earth, and to tread more lightly upon it. You can help us to a stronger remembrance of physical difficulties, but also to a re-experienced joy and sensuality in some aspects of the physical world. The rainbow bridges are getting stronger, try never to doubt that, even though there may be times of disillusionment. We are alongside you, not carrying you, or choosing for you, but moving with you, and you with us to more optimum conditions of being. My love and blessing are with you.'

Conclusion

By Gildas

'This is a time in the evolution of thought and experience where a most important key word is that of 'co-creatorship'. Certain energies have been released into the planet, and from the planet which make it essential for humanity to own this concept, and realize a true 'coming of age' in a spiritual sense.

It has never been so vitally important that humankind should fully understand its spiritual nature. Individuals endeavouring to fulfil that requirement feed their experience into the collective being of humanity so that trust, and faith can be reborn, and the power of unconditional love can be added to them.

'Coming of age' is a rite of passage, and an initiation, and is seen and celebrated as such by almost every culture and sub-culture. Yet although it may have such recognition in society and its structures, it has failed to be fully recognised in its spiritual dimensions. Though there is a ritual and marking of the moment when a young person becomes an adult and an equal, there is no complementary ritual which acknowledges spiritual responsibility.

Any initiation is not without its difficulties. Often preparation for initiation or rite of passage has been made difficult or painful, in order to call forth the qualities of courage, self reliance and stamina. Eventually initiation can become a gentler process, and in many ways this could be true in your present times. It can only be true however when there is acknowledgement of co-creatorship, a real acceptance of the divine spark within.

Part of the difficulty is that humankind is going through a very painful initiation without recognising it as such. Therefore there is a great tendency to remain stuck in the pain, to feel victims in an irreversible situation, and to assume that God is dead because there seems to be no evidence of divine intervention into the present situation. True 'coming of age' *requires* the symbolic death of the parent figures as holders of power, jurisdiction and the ability to intervene. Only then can the new adult feel the potential of self actualization, and of true dialogue with, and participation in the forming of the rules and conditions of life. So if God the parent is dead, it is a very good thing, but humanity still needs to see itself not as orphaned, but as released into creative responsibility and potential.

Access to guidance is about access to wisdom. If it is seen as such it is a truly creative journey towards co-creatorship. If it is seen as an opportunity to hand over responsibility, it can be a journey towards inaccuracy, increase in dependency, and away from the realization of unconditional love. This is basically the thesis of this book, therefore I see it as a book very much needed in these times.

The realization of unconditional love can only happen when mutually responsible beings interact together. It is a condition of mutual giving and receiving, not something which pours out from one source to be received by another. This condition or realization is essential to the progress of these times, but also manifests, when effected, an indescribably beautiful view over the future landscape.

Make no doubt there will be a future, and the capacity for that future to be positive and beautiful is not yet lost. We long to be co-creators with you, and to take the rest of the journey to true spiritual co-creatorship with you; as equal partners, with mutual respect. If anything in this book can help you to that vision, understanding or actuality then the book may be seen as a celebration. I greet the time when more of us from either dimension are celebrating in full consciousness.'

Glossary of some terms used in this book

(Listed mainly in the order in which they have been mentioned in the text.)

Earlier Maps of the Psyche: This reference is particularly to the Freudian map, which divides consciousness into three parts, similarly to the egg map of Assagioli. The areas however, are seen to be out of communication with each other, and even to exist for the purpose of blocking communication within the psyche. In comparison with the Assagioli egg diagram, the 'ID', would approximate to the Lower Unconscious; the 'EGO' to the Usual Field of Consciousness, and the Middle Unconscious, and the 'SUPER EGO' to the Higher Unconscious.

Jungian maps of consciousness, though usually circular, and denoting a wider concept of wholeness, also contain solid lines, and therefore do not *diagrammatically* give the impression of ease of movement of psychological material. In concept, Jung embraces great depth and potential for the psyche. Assagioli developed a practical and popular application for the concepts of Transpersonal Psychology, in his teaching known as Psychosynthesis. (See Chapter 1.)

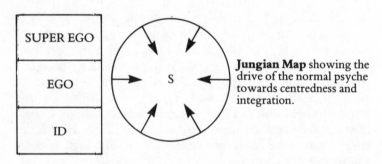

Jungian Map showing the drive of the normal psyche towards centredness and integration.

Aura: An energy field, comprising subtler 'bodies', which interpenetrates but also radiates out beyond the physical body. When seen clairvoyantly, the aura is full of light and colour. To the trained and gifted clairvoyant the shadings of colour, or patches of darkness in the auric fields can give indications as to the spiritual, mental, physical and emotional state of the individual.

Subtle Bodies: These are the bodies, again surrounding and to some extent interpenetrating the physical, which are brought into particular use when awareness expands, and the experience of higher levels of consciousness comes to the individual. The subtle bodies, together with the physical, make up the total vehicle of incarnate life. Through the subtle bodies, links with the wider being are maintained, and 'remembered'. The physical body is left behind at death, but the subtle body remain as 'clothing' for the spirit as it passes to the 'other side'. The *Etheric Body* is the closest to the physical. The total number of bodies is accepted by most sources as seven, though terminology for them varies. The terms used by Gildas, are: The Physical Body; The Etheric Body; The Astral Body; The Feeling Body; The Lower Mental Body; The Higher Mental Body, and The Soul or Causal Body.

Elementals: Tiny beings of consciousness, generally associated with plants and trees, and the natural environment. These are clairvoyantly seen as points of light or colour, or as 'fairies', 'nereids', 'sylphs', 'gnomes', 'elves', etc. Elementals are amoral but are attracted to sources of energy, or energy depletion. Therefore although amoral, they do often play a part in healing plants or animals. Since they are attracted by energy, they often involve themselves with mechanical things like cars, typewriters etc. They are part of a hierarchy, which is different from the human stream of consciousness, and which moves from the elemental life through to Devic consciousness, and then to Angelic consciousness.

Devic Beings: can be sometimes confused with angels. Often they are perceived or sensed to be very tall. They have evolved from the amorality of elemental being, into positive concern with trees, rocks, plants, power points and earth, air, fire, and water energies. They seek to bring healing and balance to these natural realms, and to the interaction of humanity with these realms.

Angelic Beings: have a higher mental consciousness, and are guardians of the earth, and humanity, working towards the sort of unity, balance and wholeness in all things which enables the true evolution and integration of Divinity.

The elemental/devic/angelic hierarchy or lifestream, may be seen as moving from the Divine consciousness towards earth, while the human stream of consciousness, which includes discarnate guides, may be seen to be moving towards reunification with the Divine. Thus the elemental/devic/angelic hierarchy, is separate from humanity. Discarnates are not angels, and angels will not take on human form or consciousness. The Guardian Angel, is thus different from the guide, or discarnate mentor.

Chakras: (See Chapter 5.) Literally 'wheels', (from Sanskrit). They are psychically receptive and active centres, interpenetrating and affecting the physical as well as the subtle bodies. Healing rays are often directed immediately into the chakras, and are certainly received there. The main chakras are often named as the crown, the brow, the throat, the heart, the solar plexus, the sacral centre and the root. They are seen psychically in a line down the centre of the body, and radiating out into the subtler bodies, and the auric field. There are many chakras in the bodies, and most are more minutely represented in energy terms in the hands, the feet, the eyes, and the ears.

Aquarian Age: (or Age of Aquarius). Astrologically, periods particularly affected by certain signs, in the evolution of collective human consciousness, and the measurement of time, last for approximately two thousand years. The cosmic zodiac runs in the opposite direction from the personal, or yearly zodiac. The incarnation of Jesus Christ, brought in the Piscean Age. We now move collectively into the Aquarian Age. In these longer time spans it is difficult to determine when an age actually begins, but the cuspal time, or time of transition from one to the other is a matter of decades rather than days, or hours. The cuspal time is powerful, and often inconsistent in its energies. Gildas teaches that we are now in the Aquarian Age, having passed the cusp during the period, March 1986–August 1988, but energies of transition will continue to affect us for some considerable time. Pisces is a water sign, with the symbol of two fishes swimming in opposite directions. Aquarius is an air sign, with a symbol of a water carrier, pouring water out onto the earth.

Anima/Animus: These are complex Jungian terms, Briefly, in each male there is the presence of the feminine, (anima), in each female the presence of the masculine, (animus). An important part of personality integration, whatever our gender, is to come to inner terms with both the masculine and the feminine principles. Since the anima and the animus are initially unconscious aspects, they can have a negative autonomy or drive. Brought into consciousness and balance they enable the inner mystical, or spiritual marriage, essential to wholeness and self-actualisation.

Karma: The spiritual laws of cause and effect. 'As you sow, so shall you reap', gives a general flavour of the meaning, but is over-simplified, and can lead to interpretations which lack compassion. The spiritual laws of karma do not lack compassion; they operate on very positive levels as well as on the negative levels. There is also group, racial, and world karma, which has a great influence on total human history and evolution. There is no simple or adequate explanation of the laws of karma, part of the journey of spiritual growth is to learn to understand and work with their complexities. Most teachings about karma are also related to belief in reincarnation.